SECOND-DEGREE
WHITE BELT
SUDOKU™

Frank Longo

Sterling Publishing Co., Inc.
New York

CONTENTS

Introduction
3

Puzzles
5

Answers
155

2   4   6   8   10   9   7   5   3   1

Martial Arts Sudoku and White Belt Sudoku
are trademarks of Sterling Publishing Co., Inc.

Published by Sterling Publishing Co., Inc.
387 Park Avenue South, New York, NY 10016
© 2005 by Sterling Publishing Co., Inc.
Distributed in Canada by Sterling Publishing
C/o Canadian Manda Group, 165 Dufferin Street
Toronto, Ontario, Canada M6K 3H6
Distributed in Great Britain by Chrysalis Books Group PLC
The Chrysalis Building, Bramley Road, London W10 6SP, England
Distributed in Australia by Capricorn Link (Australia) Pty. Ltd.
P.O. Box 704, Windsor, NSW 2756, Australia

Sterling ISBN 13: 978-1-4027-3714-5
Sterling ISBN 10: 1-4027-3714-9

For information about custom editions, special sales, premium and
corporate purchases, please contact Sterling Special Sales
Department at 800-805-5489 or specialsales@sterlingpub.com.

INTRODUCTION

To solve sudoku puzzles, all you need to know is this one simple rule:

Fill in the boxes so that the nine rows, the nine columns, and the nine 3×3 sections all contain every digit from 1 to 9.

And that's all there is to it! Using this simple rule, let's see how far we get on this sample puzzle at right. (The letters at the top and left edges of the puzzle are for reference only; you won't see them in the regular puzzles.)

	A	B	C	D	E	F	G	H	I
J									
K					2		1	8	4
L	9		5		7		2		6
M	1		4	3	9	2		7	
N				7		6			
O		7		1	4	8	9		2
P	3		2		6		8		5
Q	8	4	9		3				
R									

The first number that can be filled in is an obvious one: box EN is the only blank box in the center 3×3 section, and all the digits 1 through 9 are represented except for 5. EN must be 5.

The next box is a little trickier to discover. Consider the upper left 3×3 section of the puzzle. Where can a 4 go? It can't go in AK, BK, or CK because row K already has a 4 at IK. It can't go in BJ or BL because column B already has a 4 at BQ. It can't go in CJ because column C already has a 4 at CM. So it must go in AJ.

Another box in that same section that can now be filled is BJ. A 2 can't go in AK, BK, or CK due to the 2 at EK. The 2 at GL rules out a 2 at BL. And the 2 at CP means that a 2 can't go in CJ. So BJ must contain the 2. It is worth noting that this 2 couldn't have been placed without the 4 at AJ in place.

Many of the puzzles rely on this type of steppingstone behavior.

We now have a grid as shown.

Let's examine column A. There are four blank boxes in column A; in which blank box must the 2 be placed? It can't be AK because of the 2 in EK (and the 2 in BJ). It can't be AO because of the 2 in IO. It can't be AR because of the 2 in CP. Thus, it must be AN that has the 2.

	A	B	C	D	E	F	G	H	I
J	4	2							
K					2		1	8	4
L	9		5		7		2		6
M	1		4	3	9	2		7	
N				7	5	6			
O		7		1	4	8	9		2
P	3		2		6		8		5
Q	8	4	9		3				
R									

By the 9's in AL, EM, and CQ, box BN must be 9. Do you see how?

We can now determine the value for box IM. Looking at row M and then column I, we find all the digits 1 through 9 are represented but 8. IM must be 8.

This brief example of some of the techniques leaves us with the grid at right.

You should now be able to use what you learned to fill in CN followed by BL, then HL followed by DL and FL.

As you keep going through this puzzle, you'll find it gets easier as you fill in more. And as you keep working through the puzzles in this book, you'll find it gets easier and more fun each time. The final answer is shown below.

This book consists of 300 puzzles of easy level of difficulty.

—Frank Longo

	A	B	C	D	E	F	G	H	I
J	4	2							
K					2		1	8	4
L	9		5		7		2		6
M	1		4	3	9	2		7	8
N	2	9		7	5	6			
O		7		1	4	8	9		2
P	3		2		6		8		5
Q	8	4	9		3				
R									

	A	B	C	D	E	F	G	H	I
J	4	2	1	6	8	3	5	9	7
K	7	3	6	5	2	9	1	8	4
L	9	8	5	4	7	1	2	3	6
M	1	5	4	3	9	2	6	7	8
N	2	9	8	7	5	6	4	1	3
O	6	7	3	1	4	8	9	5	2
P	3	1	2	9	6	7	8	4	5
Q	8	4	9	2	3	5	7	6	1
R	5	6	7	8	1	4	3	2	9

1

1	2	3	4	5	6			
				3	9			1
8	6						3	
					8		6	
		5				1		
	4		3					
	7						1	2
3			2	7				
			9	8	5	3	7	6

2

3	7		5					
			3		8	4	5	
6						7	8	
					3	6		
2	6		7		4		9	5
		9	2					
	1	4						9
	9	6	1		7			
					9		6	1

3

3	6		7					1
	2			9			7	
	4							
6		2		4				
	3		6		8		5	
				5		9		3
							2	
	7			6			9	
4					5		8	6

4

1				6	7	2		
		5	2			6	1	3
	3	1	7			8	4	
	8						2	
		2	4			5	7	3
6	5	7				4	9	
		9	8	5				4

5

6	4		1	7				
		1			5	3		
9	8		3					
	9			3				
1		4				8		2
				2			3	
					3		4	8
		8	6			1		
				9	4		2	7

6

		9	2	1			4	
6			5			7	1	3
							6	
		5	7				9	
		2				8		
	6				9	1		
	9							
7	5	3			8			6
	1			3	5	4		

7

	2				4			5
5	6	1			3	8		
							3	
7			4			3		8
				2				
6		8			7			1
	4							
		9	3			2	7	6
1			9				4	

8

5		6						
3			7		6			
	8	1	9					
9					2	7	4	
		3		9		8		
	5	4	1					6
					4	6	2	
			3		8			7
						3		8

	4					7		
	5	8	9				4	
2				5	6			
		1		4				7
		9				8		
4				2		1		
			5	7				8
	6				2	5	7	
		7					9	

			5		3			
		4	2			5		7
			7				9	
	4			1	6		7	3
2		1				9		6
6	7		9	3			4	
	6			8				
9		3			5	7		
			3		4			

Puzzle 1-1:

		6				3		
	5	9	4		3			1
2		3			7			
				7	2			
3		7				9		4
			5	9				
			1			8		7
5			6		9	2	1	
		2				5		

Puzzle 1-2:

2	6			8		9		
9		8	2		7			3
	7	9	1		3		4	
		2				5		
	8		5		9	3	1	
6			3		1	2		4
		1		5			9	6

4		8				1	9	
1				7			4	
					1		6	
3			6	2				
			8		9			
				4	7			5
	8		1					
	9			8				7
	3	4				8		6

1					6		7	
2	4				3			8
					9	4		2
3	9							
7		6				5		4
							8	3
8		3	2					
9			8				5	6
	2		9					1

1 / 5

	7	4	6	8			5	
		6	2	3				
8							4	
	5						6	
4		1		6		3		7
	3						1	
	4							1
				9	3	5		
	6			2	5	4	9	

1 / 6

	9		1	7	2			6
	2				6	5		
		6	4					
5	4				3			
		1		9		3		
			7				5	8
					7	4		
		9	2				7	
7			3	8	1		2	

	6				2	4		3
5		2			7			
		8	3		6	1		
		9					3	
			7		4			
	5					6		
		7	4		3	9		
			9			2		4
8		4	2				5	

		6			2	5		9
					5	6		
	9				1	8	4	3
7					3			
		1				9		
			8					2
2	1	3	4				9	
		7	1					
6		8	7			4		

Puzzle 19

	8	4					1	
			3	1		8		
	6				5		3	7
		6		8	4			
	7	9				4	8	
			6	5		9		
6	1		5				4	
		7		2	3			
	5					1	7	

Puzzle 20

	9							
			9	8		3	6	
		3		6		2		
4			1	2				
1		8		3		7		6
				7	8			9
		5		4		8		
	4	6		1	2			
							1	

			5			4	7	2
			4			6		
2	5				6		3	
	7				5	2		
	4			8			5	
		9	2				6	
	1		9				2	7
		3			7			
6	9	7			1			

				1	9			5
		2				8	9	
6			4	2				
	7				2	4		3
	2			3			7	
4		6	5				8	
				4	7			6
	5	7				9		
2			9	5				

Puzzle 2/3

		1		7			4	
	3	9	8		4			6
		8						
	8		4			6		
1		2		3		4		5
		6			2		7	
						2		
2			5		9	7	3	
	7			6		5		

Puzzle 2/4

	7	8	1		4			
	1							8
4			2	6	8			
					5	2		9
5			3		7			1
7		4	6					
			4	3	9			6
2							9	
			5		2	3	8	

		6	9	5				
	1				7	9	6	
	4			8				
1		2		3	8	4		5
6		9	1	4		7		3
				6			3	
	9	8	5				4	
				9	4	2		

	3	5			8	4		
			6					
9	1	4				5		
2	4		7					
	9	3				2	4	
					2		3	5
		2				1	5	8
				6				
		1	2			6	9	

2 / 7

3						9		
				4				
5	9	4		3		2		1
	2				7	3	5	
6								7
	8	3	2				6	
2		9		6		7	1	5
				7				
		6						2

2 / 8

		1				8	5	
				3	6			2
	4	2			1	3		
9	8						2	
		3	2		5	6		
	2						9	1
		4	3			9	6	
1			5	4				
	3	5				7		

	6							
7						6		9
1		2	9	3		4		5
8		4	5			9		
				8				
		5			3	2		4
9		6		7	8	3		1
2		8						6
							5	

	5						4	8
				4		3		
	4	1					9	5
	7		4		9			
1	3		6		7		5	2
			5		3		8	
5	2					6	7	
		9		7				
6	1						3	

Puzzle 3/1:

	6		4		9			
5		4		3		2		1
								4
6					5	4		
	4		6		8		2	
		8	7					9
2								
3		1		7		5		6
			5		1		3	

Puzzle 3/2:

3	1				5		6	
7			4	3		1		
	2						9	
			5	4				
2	3		7		1		8	5
				8	9			
	4						7	
		2		9	4			3
	5		6				2	4

	6						3	
1		2		3		4		5
		5					9	2
			4			7		8
3		6			7			
7	2					3		
9		3		2		1		7
	8						2	

5					8		1	4
				4	9		5	
4	1							3
		5	8					
3		1		9		6		7
					7	5		
2							8	9
	4		9	7				
1	3		2					6

3 / 5

5		4		3		2		1
	2		6		9		4	
		1						
		7	1					
	9		2		8		1	
					3	9		
						4		
	7		4		6		3	
1		3		5		8		6

3 / 6

1			2	6				9
					1		5	
2			9		8			4
	5						4	1
3				8				5
7	9						8	
4			6		2			8
	6		7					
5				1	9			6

1		2		3		4		5
					6		8	2
	1			5		6	2	
3			1		8			7
	2	8		7			5	
8	3		7					
6		7		1		5		3

9		4						1
		5			7			
		6		3	2			5
		7			8			6
	9		4		1		2	
8			5			1		
4			6	1		5		
			7			6		
6						8		3

1	2	3	4				7	
				1	2	3	4	
6			8					
3	9	1						
	5						8	
						1	3	4
					4			3
	3	9	1	2				
	4				7	5	1	2

						9		
9	8	7	6		4			
	5			9	8	7	6	
				3	9			4
	3						7	
6			2	5				
	6	2	5	7			1	
			1		6	2	5	7
		1						

Puzzle 4-1

	9							6
	8			5		2	4	
	7		4	1		9		
	6	2				3		
		9	5		3	4		
		8				1	5	
		7		3	1		9	
	4	6		7			2	
9							3	

Puzzle 4-2

						1		
1	8	6			9		3	
		5		1	3	2		
		2		7	6		1	
				9				
	7		2	4		9		
		1	8	6		3		
	9		1			6	2	8
		3						

4 3

	9			8		5		3
					5		8	1
7	8		4					6
			1			9		7
2		4			6			
3					1		7	2
5	7		3					
1		6		4			3	

4 4

		5	3		1			4
						7		3
6		9			7		2	
1			7					
		3				6		
					5			1
	6		2			4		9
4		8						
2			1		6	5		

Puzzle 45

			1	7		3		5
1					3	2		
					5			6
8		2				7	6	
3								4
	4	1				9		2
4			7					
		6	3					9
5		7		1	8			

Puzzle 46

	8	1	2	4				
4	3		6		7			5
		3	9	6				7
	2						6	
6				3	5	8		
7			1		6		5	8
			8	3	6	4		

4 / 7

	8	9					3	
	1		8					
				9		2		
	9	1	3				5	4
4				8				3
3	7				5	1	8	
		8		5				
					2		4	
	4					7	6	

4 / 8

	9	6					5	
5		3	8					
	1		9	5		8		3
	3			4		9	7	
	5	4		9			1	
3		7		1	9		4	
					5	6		2
	2					7	3	

		2			1			5
7	1				4	8		
	9		8		6		2	
	2			9				
		1				2		
				8			6	
	4		2		9		5	
		8	6				3	4
3			5			1		

	5	8						4
		9	2	6				5
		1				9		6
	2			7	6		4	
	6						3	
	4		1	9			5	
7		4				5		
5				3	2	8		
3						4	6	

						3	5	1
			4	6	2	9		
7	9	8				4		
					5	2		8
				7				
8		4	3					
		1				5	3	2
		2	1	8	9			
4	6	7						

3						1	4	7
1				8		3		
5					3	9		
	4		6	3			1	
	2						9	
	6			4	2		5	
		7	8					9
		8		6				1
4	1	9						2

1	3	5						
			2	4	6			
					5	9	8	7
	8		7		3		2	5
7	2		8		1		3	
4	6	8	1					
			4	8	7			
						4	9	8

	3			9	1	4		8
	9	5			7	3		
					8	6		7
		3	4		9	8		
4		8	2					
		9	7			1	3	
7		4	9	1			5	

5/5

7		1		3	6			9
		3	5			7		
6			4			5		
						2	1	
3				8				7
	1	7						
		2			5			4
		8			7	1		
4			9	1		3		6

5/6

3	5		7			6		
			9	8	3		4	
5	2				6		8	
		1	5		8	9		
	4		1				5	7
	9		3	4	1			
		8			7		3	1

Puzzle 57

8						3		
	6		2					
		9	3	1	6			
	3		6	2				
	2	5		3		6	8	
				4	7		1	
			9	5	3	1		
					2		5	
		6						4

Puzzle 58

				8			2	
	8		3					
6			4		1		5	8
9							7	1
1	2		8		5		9	4
3	4							6
5	6		1		8			7
					6		3	
	7			3				

8				5				
		1		4			9	
7			9			6	3	4
						4	2	7
2	3						5	6
4	5	6						
6	7	3			8			5
	9			6		2		
				9				3

2	3		8	1				
4	5							
6	7	8	9		5	2		
	9		7				3	
	1				3		8	
		5	2		8	3	9	1
							6	2
				7	9		5	8

6 / 1

1	4				5		6	
2	5					4		
3	7		8	9			5	
				4				6
			7		9			
7				2				
	9			6	8		3	2
		3					4	5
	1		9				7	8

6 / 2

9					6	7		1
7					4	2	6	
5					8			
3		2					1	
1								7
	4					5		8
			5					4
	5	7	6					2
4		1	2					3

6/3

1	8	2					7	
3	9							
5	6			9				
7				6	9	2		
9			5		2			4
		3	7	1				5
				4			6	2
							3	7
	7					8	5	9

6/4

9	7	5	3	1				6
			2	9				4
		6						
		9				6	5	
		7		8		9		
	1	2				7		
						4		
3				6	5			
5				7	1	2	3	9

						5	1	9
					3	2		8
9			4		5	3		6
	9		1	6				7
7				8	9		5	
4		1	2		6			3
2		9	7					
8	6	3						

2	3		4		7			
6					2	7		
8		7		3				
	2	1		6			9	
9								5
	7			1		4	6	
				5		6		7
		8	6					3
			8		9		2	1

							3	7
				5		9	2	
		3			7	4	1	
	1			3	6			9
		6		9		7		
9			7	8			6	
	8	5	6			1		
	3	4		2				
1	2							

2					7	8		
6				4				
9		7			5	2	3	
		9	8					
8			4			6		3
						3	5	
	4	8	6			7		2
				8				1
		1	3					9

69

				7	1	8		
8			3					4
1				8	6	7	2	3
				4	2			
	2						7	
		5	2					
4	7	8	5	1				6
2					8			7
		6	7	3				

70

	4		9		6			
		6			3	5		4
5	1		2			9		
	7			9				
		8				1		
				6			3	
		7			2		1	3
2		4	1			6		
			6		7		4	

Puzzle 7/1

1	2	3		8				
			4	5	6		2	
						7	8	9
			6				4	2
3								6
2	1				8			
5	9	1						
	4		5	3	9			
				1		9	6	5

Puzzle 7/2

1	2	3	9					
			3	2	7			
7							2	4
3	6							
	9		2		5		1	
							8	7
5	7							8
			5	3	9			
					2	4	6	5

1	2	3						
		4			1	9	2	8
	8		5					
		1						2
	7	5	8		4	1	6	
3						4		
					7		3	
4	6	2	3			5		
						2	1	4

		9			2		1	
	8			4	1		9	
			9			2	3	
7	1					8		
		3	1		6	7		
		6					2	1
	5	8			9			
	3		8	1			7	
	7		2			5		

	9				5	8		
1					7	3		
			9	4				
4	8	7			1		3	
3								5
	5		3			7	2	4
				3	9			
		2	7					8
		6	4				9	

	6							9
		9		4		2		5
4	2			3				6
	1				3			
	4		2	9	7		1	
			8				5	
3				1			2	8
7		4		8		5		
1							9	

					3			9
9	3			6				5
	4	2				6	3	
			4	5		7		
4			2		1			8
		5		7	8			
	2	8				3	7	
6				3			8	4
3			6					

	8					9	4	
		9	2	6				8
1			8			7		
				3	7		8	
			5		8			
	7		9	1				
		1			9			3
2				8	6	1		
	5	6					7	

79

1	2	3		9		4	5	6
	7			3	6			
								9
8	1			6				
			1		9			
				5			1	2
3								
			2	4			9	
4	5	6		7		1	2	3

80

1		3			6			
5	8			2			7	
	9		3		8		6	
			5		3	6		
				1				
		4	2		9			
	2		9		7		5	
	6			3			9	4
			6			7		3

		4			8	3	6	
	7				6			
				2			4	
		5	1	8			3	
1		3		5		7		9
	9			7	4	1		
	1			6				
			8				9	
	5	6	9			8		

1	9							
							4	
		4	2	6	8		1	
8	6				7			
9		7		5		3		1
			4				6	5
	3		5	7	1	9		
	8							
							5	6

8 / 3

	8	5			7	3		
2	1		4					
3		4				6		
9					2		8	7
8	4		3					5
		8				4		1
					6		5	9
		1	5			8	3	

8 / 4

					3		1	9
				4			6	
		9		6			2	3
3		5		8				1
			4		5			
9				2		5		4
7	9			5		3		
	5			3				
4	2		1					

1						8		
	2			6		9		
		3		2		1		7
			4	3				2
	6		8	5	7		9	
5				1	6			
3		1		8		7		
		4		7			8	
		7						9

8	2							
		6		4				
			1	2	3		9	
	8	1				7		3
5		2	3		7	8		1
4		3				9	2	
	1		4	5	6			
				1		4		
							8	5

Puzzle 8/7

	8		4			2	1	
		9						
7			1	6			9	5
		7			5			9
			2		1			
4			6			1		
8	4			3	7			6
						3		
	3	2			6		4	

Puzzle 8/8

		7	8	2				
		6			7		1	
	1					2		5
	6							2
				3				
5							9	
2		9					4	
	7		1			3		
				5	3	8		

	2		1		5			
7		8	2				6	
		4	3	8				9
8		2		4				
				5				
				6		2		5
1				2	7	9		
	9				8	6		3
			6		9		5	

		7					4	
			3			5		
6	8						2	
1	2	3			9			
8			4	5	6			1
			1			7	8	9
	3						5	6
		8			5			
	4					9		

Puzzle 91

7		2		8				9
8				3		6		
1				7		3		
	4				3			5
		7	9		6	8		
2			8				9	
		1		9				6
		5		1				8
3				6		1		7

Puzzle 92

							1	4
1	8				4		3	5
	4				3		6	7
6	1			3				
			1		2			
				8			7	1
9	6		4				8	
8	5		7				2	6
2	7							

	2		3		4			
8		4			2	1		5
	9				8			6
			8					
	5		9		7		2	
					1			
9			7				1	
1		3	2			7		4
			4		3		9	

5		4	3			2		
				1		4	6	3
							9	1
	5		2					
9			8	3	5			6
					7		2	
4	8							
1	3	5		8				
		7			4	3		8

5			6		2			
9							1	6
	2	1		8	9			
				7		5	3	
8			1		5			4
	5	2		4				
			2	9		6	5	
1	7							9
			7		4			1

		7				3		1
2			6			8		
9							4	5
	5		4		3			9
		2				4		
7			8		2		6	
6	7							4
		5			4			2
4		3				1		

				2		1		
		3		1		5	7	
1	4		6				8	9
8					9	3	6	
	3	2	7					1
5	1				6		2	3
	2	9		7		6		
		4		9				

	3					5		6
				2	9	8		
			6	4		2	9	
		6			2		3	
3								8
	2		3			6		
	6	3		9	1			
		9	7	8				
4		5					8	

2		8	6	7				9
			4			1		7
	4		9				2	
		9		1		2		
1								4
		2		6		5		
	1				9		4	
3		7			6			
9				3	5	8		2

8			2				7	1
7							3	
			1	5		6		4
9	7			2		3		
				4				
		8		3			2	7
3		7		1	6			
	9							3
5	8				4			6

					4			6
	6		8			4		
9							7	1
	8			5	9		3	
4				3				5
	7		6	2			1	
2	3							7
		5			6		9	
8			1					

6				3	4	2		8
	1						7	4
						9		
				1			8	
4	2		5		8		3	9
	8			9				
		2						
8	4						5	
7		6	3	2				1

Puzzle 103

7				9	8	3		1
						6	2	5
4		1		5			7	9
			4	8	7			
8	7			3		4		6
9	2	7						
6		8	1	7				4

Puzzle 104

			1			2	8	
		5		3	6		4	
		4	7			1		
							2	
	9	1	8		5	6	3	
	6							
		6			7	9		
	4		3	6		5		
	5	7			8			

						2		
		6	9	8	7			
3		1				4	8	
	5		4	6	8			
			1	5	9		7	
	9	4				8		1
			6	1	2	5		
		5						

			6	5	8		9	
				7			1	8
			2		4		6	
			8				3	7
4								2
7	9				6			
	7		4		5			
5	4			3				
	3		9	8	7			

	7	6			2	3	9	
3	4				1			
						8		7
	1				6			
6		5				7		9
			7				1	
2		1						
			6				8	4
	6	7	8			5	3	

			1	9			2	
	4				7	1	9	
			4					7
7			2			5	1	
	1						3	
	2	6			5			9
2					4			
	5	9	7				4	
	7			6	9			

1		7		8		2		
			7		2			
	2		1				3	8
		9		5				
6	4	2				5	7	3
				7		4		
5	1				4		8	
			5		1			
		4		3		1		5

3		5	2				6	
		8	3			9		5
			1		7			3
	9					4		
	2	6				1	3	
		1					9	
6			4		2			
2		9			1	6		
	1				6	2		9

	4		6	3				8
9			4	7		3	2	
						9		
		1				2		7
	7			8			5	
8		9				4		
		4						
	8	7		6	4			2
6				5	3		4	

			3	5	4		9	
			8			3		
8				7		1	6	4
	8							
5	2			6			3	8
							2	
1	4	7		8				6
		3			5			
	5		6	9	7			

2					4	3		
6		4	3				1	
1				8				
9	3	6	4					
					5	6	9	8
				4				5
	1				7	8		9
		5	2					1

				6				8
	8	6	5	9		7		
		5			2			9
	4					5		
		7				3		
		3					7	
3			9			6		
		8		5	6	9	2	
4				8				

	7	3						
		1	8		4	6		
	2		6	1				
			2				5	
5		6				1		3
	1			5				
				3	1		7	
		4	5		8	2		
						3	8	

	2		3			9		1
4				1			7	
				2	8			
3	9					6	4	
7				4				9
	6	4					2	5
			8	7				
	7			3				4
5		1			2		3	

		2	7					3
1						7	4	6
	9		3					
		4		5			8	7
		8		9		5		
5	3			7		6		
					6		7	
3	7	1						9
2					7	1		

							8	
	5						2	7
	7	9				5		6
	1		9		2			8
8			7		5			4
3			8		4		1	
2		5				8	7	
9	3						4	
	8							

	1	2						
	3		8			9		
4	5						3	
			6	3		7		
6	7			8			1	3
		8		7	2			
	2						8	7
		7			9		6	
						5	9	

8	1			2		5	4	
	4	3	1	8				
9								
2		4			7		6	
	8		6			7		2
								4
			7	6	1	9		
	3	7		9			5	6

					4			
4	9	5			2			
		3				7	9	
8		2			9		7	
			8	3	5			
	5		6			8		9
	6	8				3		
			7			4	6	2
			2					

	5		3				8	
		6			4	7		
			8			1		3
						8	7	
	1	7	4		5	2	3	
	9	5						
5		8			3			
		1	7			3		
	3				2		6	

Puzzle 1-2-3

	1			3	7	6		
3	2							
		9			4	7		
6		2		9				
			2		1			
				7		3		6
		5	8			1		
							5	7
		4	7	5			6	

Puzzle 1-2-4

	9	5		7				6
7				2		3		
1					6			
	7		6	8				3
			7		3			
6				5	1		2	
			9					1
		4		1				8
3				6		7	5	

				9	1		8	
	5			4	6			3
		1						5
3		5	6					
4		6				5		7
					3	9		4
6						2		
5			2	3			7	
	4		1	6				

			3		6			7
	5		8	7				2
9	8							
	9			3		8		
		5				1		
		1		2			4	
							1	8
4				8	2		5	
2			6		5			

127

8		5	4				9	2
	9		7			5		
				5				
1		3	9					6
			8		6			
4					3	8		5
				6				
		8			7		5	
9	3				4	7		1

128

							7	
		2		4		1		8
7	9				3	2		
	8			3	5			4
3	2						1	5
6			9	1			3	
		8	3				4	1
9		1		7		3		
	7							

				8		4		
2	4			7			6	
5			2					3
6		2	8			9		
	9						7	
		4			9	6		1
8					1			5
	5			2			9	7
		9		5				

	4	8	5				7	
		1				5		4
7					4		8	
	8			6	2	7	5	
	7	9	3	8			6	
	3		8					6
9		4				8		
	6				7	4	9	

Puzzle 131

		9	5	2				
1		7						
	3	6	4	7	8			
7						6		
			7	9	4			
		5						9
			8	5	3	9	4	
						2		3
				6	9	7		

Puzzle 132

				1				7
	2	3	4					
8							9	3
		8		9			4	1
1				7				9
3	6			5		7		
9	1							4
					5	9	1	
6				2				

2	6			5	9	3		8
8		9			3			
7							4	
		6		4			7	
	5			1		6		
	9							6
			3			8		7
3		8	5	7			9	2

6			1		2		8	
		3	9				1	
	2			5	3		4	
9		2						
8								6
						8		3
	6		5	9			2	
	9				1	7		
	5		4		6			1

Puzzle 1 3 5

		8		2				
		2				4	3	
			8	6				5
					3	8		
8	4	7				3	9	1
		3	1					
9				8	5			
	7	4				6		
				4		2		

Puzzle 1 3 6

		1					3	5
6	9							
3		2	5	4				
	3			1			6	
8		7		2		4		3
	4			8			7	
				3	8	5		2
							9	7
7	5					3		

137

		7	8	2		9	3	
		3		9				7
		4						
	2			4		7		
5		9		6		8		3
		4		5			2	
					9			
3				1		5		
	5	6		8	3	1		

138

9		5		1	7			
						4		8
3	8		2					
		9	7					6
5			1		6			9
7					3	5		
					2		5	7
2		6						
			5	4		6		1

Puzzle 139

	8		7				1	2
		3						
			2		3	4		
				8			5	6
9	6						7	3
8	2			7				
		6	9		1			
						6		
5	7				8		4	

Puzzle 140

				4		6	7	
					2		5	
	2			7	6			8
				6				5
6		4				9		7
1				8				
8			3	2			1	
	7		6					
	4	5		1				

	1		9	7				
			2		6		7	9
						6		
		7				2	6	
9				6				8
	4	2				9		
		4						
8	2		4		3			
				9	1		3	

		4		9				5
			6				4	8
6	2		4					
			7				5	2
			5	8	9			
5	8				2			
					4		8	9
4	6				3			
9				5		1		

5		2			7			
4	9	7	8	1				
	1		3					
2					4			
	5	9		7		8	2	
			9					5
					5		7	
				8	9	4	5	1
			2			9		8

	7		2					4
	9		4	8				1
		2						7
		8			9			
			1		4			
			5			3		
3						2		
8				7	2		1	
5					6		8	

Puzzle 145

9	5				2	8	3	
1								
3			5				2	
			8	1			4	
7				6				8
	9			2	5			
	4				8			9
								4
	7	3	4				5	6

Puzzle 146

				4	1			
1			3					6
5		8	6					
2				6		7	3	
3			2		4			8
	7	1		5				4
					6	2		5
4					9			1
			4	8				

		4						1
		8	6		7		4	
5								2
2	8			5				
6		7		2		4		9
				8			5	7
7								8
	4		5		1	3		
9						1		

2	5	3			8		4	
							7	
7			4		5		3	9
			3		7		6	
8								3
	2		5		9			
9	7		2		3			4
	3							
	6		9			3	8	7

149

			5					
	6		1		3	9	2	
3		8	2			5		6
	9	6						8
				7				
7						2	5	
5		1			8	4		2
	8	4	7		2		1	
					4			

150

			7			1		
1		3	8					
7	8			1	2			3
	6	8	1			9		
9								6
		2			5	7	1	
3			6	4			9	1
					1	3		7
		4			7			

151

		8					5	
		7	6					
		1	7	5				8
3	9	4						
			5		1			
						6	4	2
1				2	3	8		
					4	5		
	4					9		

152

			7	9		4	1	
		7				9		3
		4						
		5			9			2
			1	2	8			
9			3			7		
						8		
4		1				3		
	8	2		3	6			

		2				6		
9					3			
	6	4		7			8	
	2				8	3		
8			4		5			1
		1	6				4	
	3			4		9	5	
			3					4
		8				7		

2	7			4				8
			5				7	
	9	4					6	
3	5			6				
	6		8		7		2	
				9			8	6
	8					2	4	
	3				5			
7				1			5	9

Puzzle 155

5	4	3	2	1		8		
	1		9				6	5
		6						
					2		9	
		4		9		3		
	5		6					
						6		
8	7				9		5	
		5		7	1	9	4	8

Puzzle 156

	8			5	4	3	2	1
			9		2			
		3						9
			7				5	4
5				1				3
3	9				8			
4						1		
			1		5			
6	1	5	3	9			8	

				6	9	4	3	5
9				4			1	7
							9	
		5	6	7				
	6		2		4		8	
			1	8	7			
	5							
6	7			8				1
1	2	3	4	5				

3	7	9	4	5				1
			8				3	
		1					5	6
					5	7		
				3				
		4	7					
6	5					8		
	1				8			
8				1	2	3	4	5

159

		5		7	2			4
		4						8
					5	1		
	8	1						
5	6		9		8		7	2
						8	3	
		8	5					
6						5		
7			6	4		2		

160

	8						1	
2					6	4		8
			3			7		
				5		6		
4	9	6				3	5	7
		8		6				
		5		2				
1		7	5					2
	3						9	

	2				9		5	
					3	8		4
		4			5		2	7
		7				6		
2	8						7	3
		3				1		
4	9		5			2		
6		2	4					
	1		9				6	

			2		1	6		
			9			2		
	8	7		4		1		
9			7			5		
6								7
		8			3			2
		3		9		7	1	
		4			8			
		9	6		5			

8						2		4
2			6	4				
3			2		5		6	
9		2		7				
7								2
				5		3		8
	7		8		9			5
				1	7			6
6		8						7

				2	8		6	
	9		6		1	7		
3		6				2		
		7			5	6	9	
				9				
	1	5	2			3		
		8				1		2
		2	7		3		8	
	5		8	1				

2			7			8		
			1		4			6
	3			8		4		
		5			3		7	
	1			5			4	
	7		6			5		
		3		6			5	
8			3		2			
		4			1			7

	6			2				
							7	3
8	9		6			4		5
			2	5			4	
1		7		4		9		6
	4			6	7			
2		9			6		3	8
6	8							
				9			6	

2				6		9		8
			9				1	
7	4						2	
8	3							
	5	1				4	8	
							3	1
	6						7	4
	9				3			
5		4		8				6

5					4			1
6				9	1			
9		8			5	2		
		6			3		9	
8								3
	7		8			6		
		9	3			8		7
			9	2				4
2			4					9

169

	6			5				4
	7	3	2					
		4			6			9
		7	9			5		3
			5		8			
5		2			1	9		
7			3			4		
					4	3	5	
4				1			9	

170

1		9	3		7			
3			1	6				
		2			4		6	
						7	4	9
7								5
4	8	6						
	3		7			1		
				9	2			6
			8			3	4	7

				8				6
1	5	6						
	2		6					7
7		4						5
	9			3			7	
6						4		9
5					7		3	
						8	9	4
8				2				

			3		7			
1				9		8		4
	4		2					5
	9				5	4	6	
	6	4	1				3	
6					4		8	
7		2		5				1
			9		8			

173

	2	7					4	
5			2	4				
		3					6	5
			2	4	9			6
	1	4				3	2	
9		2	6	3				
2	4					1		
				1	9			2
	6					4	8	

174

			4		7	3	9	
		9	3					
	3	5		9	1			8
1						6		4
9								1
5		6						2
2			1	4		8	6	
					5	2		
	5	1	2		6			

2	4		5					
8						3		
	5	9		7	4			1
6					5			2
			2	4	3			
4			6					9
1			4	2		9	7	
		2						4
					1		2	8

1				2	6	8		
			4				3	
2				1	9		5	4
							7	
	6			8			1	
	2							
3	7		8	5				1
	1				4			
		5	7	9				6

				4		8		
4				3		7	6	1
5						4		2
7		4	6					
		5		8		1		
					9	3		7
2		7						5
9	5	1		6				4
		3		1				

	3		4	5		2		1
			3	8	1			
	9							
	7					6		5
3	5						1	4
2		1				3		
						4		
			6	1	3			
8		3		9	4		7	

	3	6			9			
7	9		6					2
5		2						6
		3	2				4	
8		7				3		1
	6				8	2		
6						4		5
3					5		2	8
			9			6	1	

	1	8	9		4		5	
					1			
5	3							6
	6		2				3	5
1								9
7	5				6		8	
8							7	1
			5					
	2		1		7	9	6	

			9	1				7
6			3		7		4	
			8					2
	5		8				7	4
9								1
7	1				9		5	
4				6				
	6		7		5			9
1				9	4			

5			1	2				
	3			8		4		
	8	9						7
	7		2					8
	2		8		6		5	
8					3		6	
1						9	2	
		2		4			3	
				6	2			1

Puzzle 183:

8		7						
	6	3			4			
9					8		3	1
4	5				3	8		
		9				5		
		2	9				6	4
1	4		7					8
			4			7	1	
						4		6

Puzzle 184:

4		5			7	8		
						6		2
	9				3			7
3						7	6	
			6		5			
	2	9						1
5			8				4	
8		2						
		1	2			3		5

96

	7							
		8		6		5		
	3	9		5			4	8
1	8		5			4		
7				9				3
		2			3		8	7
5	2			3		7	6	
		4		7		3		
							2	

	1				8	4		
6			2	4	7	5		9
			9					
	2					8		
			7	8	6			
		3					7	
					4			
4		9	6	2	1			8
		6	8				9	

Puzzle 187

	6		3		7			
2					5	8		
	5						1	
				6			9	3
8		9		4		1		6
7	3			9				
	1						8	
		4	9					2
			8		6		5	

Puzzle 188

	9	7			8			4
		8	6		9	2		
				2				7
				3		7		6
3								8
7		9		5				
1				6				
		6	3		4	1		
5			7			4	6	

	5			1				3
	1		4	2				
8	2				5		9	1
2				3	7			
			8	9				7
4	7		3				2	9
				8	4		1	
6				7			4	

	9	2	3			4		5
4								
		1		4			8	9
			5					
	7		4	3	2		6	
				9				
8	1			6		9		
								6
6		3			4	1	2	

8	2	7	4					3
		1	8			7	2	
			2					5
7		6		8				
			6		4			
				9		3		1
1					2			
	4	9				6	2	
2					8	4	5	7

		3		7		8		
	8		3				1	
	1		8	2				3
3		2				7	6	
				5				
	4	5				2		9
9				4	7		3	
	7				3		2	
		8		9		5		

5				1				
4	3	1						5
	7	2					1	8
	8		9	7				
		6	5		8	9		
				2	4		3	
8	6					1	4	
1						5	8	7
				8				2

4				3				6
						1	4	
	3				7		8	9
		2		7		9		
	1		9		3		6	
		4		1		7		
1	6		4				5	
	5	7						
8				5				1

7		3		2		8		
8	4			9				
			5		8			
9		8	4				1	
	5				9	7		2
			6		7			
			3				5	6
		6		1		9		8

					4		3	7
		3			8			5
	1			9				2
		4					1	
	5		2	6	1		4	
	8					2		
7				4			9	
4			8			6		
6	2		5					

	7	1			6		3	
8	4			2				
			1	8			7	6
						2	4	1
5								3
3	1	4						
1	6			9	7			
				6			5	7
	3		4			9	6	

					9		7	2
	7		8				9	
2	9	5				3		1
					3	7		
	8		1		4		2	
		9	2					
8		2				6	1	9
	6				1		4	
9	5		6					

Puzzle 199

8		2	5					4
		3		8				
					2	3		7
			6		1			5
4	1			7			9	6
7			2		8			
2		6	8					
				6		7		
9					3	5		8

Puzzle 200

7	6			5	8		9	
	4	1			9	5		
		5						2
	9		1					
		8	9		7	1		
					2		7	
6						8		
		4	6			2	3	
	1		8	2			5	7

1				3	4		9	2
8	9		7					
				2			1	
9	4				7			
	3						2	
			9				5	1
	8			9				
					8		7	9
3	2		5	7				6

6	1							
	2		4		9			
	3			1	5		2	
9	4					5	6	
	5			8			3	
	6	1					4	2
	7		8	4			1	
			3		6		7	
							5	3

	3							
		1				2		3
5		4		1	2	8		6
4						5		
	2		1		7		8	
		9						1
3		6	8	2		1		9
9		5				7		
							6	

2	8			9			3	
		7					1	9
	3		4			8		
	5			3				
			9	7	4			
				5			2	
		5			2		7	
3	1					6		
	2			4			9	3

205

	9	8	3					
					5			
						4	8	
1		5		8		9		
7				2				5
		4		6		2		3
	1	6						
			6					
					1	7	3	

206

				7	3		2	
	6	1	4				8	
		2	9					6
5	4	7				8		
		8				7	3	5
7					6	5		
	8				5	2	4	
	1		8	2				

5			3				2	
		1	5	7				
7	2				4		1	
			8		3	9		
2				9				6
		5	4		6			
	5		1				6	3
				6	8	5		
	1				5			9

	9		1	5				
2		6	9					
3	5	4				1		
4		1						
		5		2		8		
						9		6
		2				5	6	8
					5	7		3
				8	7		2	

7		3	2			8		
				9			7	
				6		3	4	
1		5			9			7
		7				6		
9			3			1		4
	8	4		1				
	9			2				
		1			4	9		8

2		1	8	9	5			
						5		
7	5			4				
		8	6		4			1
	3						7	
5			7		8	9		
				2			9	3
		9						
			4	8	9	1		2

Puzzle 211

4								5
2		1	4	6			8	
8					2		3	
7		4	6	9				
				1				
				2	4	9		8
	4		3					2
	2			4	9	5		6
6								1

Puzzle 212

1	3	5	7	9				
				5	3			
		4						
5			9			8		
	2		5		4		3	
		7			1			6
						3		
			2	4				
				6	7	2	4	8

2 1 3

1	2	3					9	
4	5					6		
	8			3				4
	7			4	1			
6			5		3			8
			9	6			4	
3				9			2	
		2					5	1
	4					3	8	9

2 1 4

2	4	6		5		9	3	
3	5		9		4			
7		9						
			7			8		3
6		1			2			
						5		8
			6		5		4	9
	9	5		7		6	1	2

2	3						1	
4	5	7	3					
6				2	5			
1						7	3	
5			2		3			1
	7	6						8
			9	5				4
					2	3	7	5
	1						6	2

		9	6	8				
						2		8
2					5	6		
5		2	8					3
		1	2	3	4	5		
3					7	8		4
		7	1					2
9		3						
				5	6	9		

Puzzle 217

							7	
1				8				9
2	8		4		1			3
8	9							
		4	2	6	9	5		
							9	6
9			5		7		2	1
7				1				4
	2							

Puzzle 218

4						8		1
3	1			5				6
		8			3	5	9	
			8			7		
			6	2	1			
		6			4			
	5	2	3			6		
6				1			5	8
9		3						2

	6	9		1			3	
8					2		7	
5			3		6	8		
						4		
	9	4				2	6	
		1						
		8	9		7			6
	5		8					9
	3			6		1	2	

		5	4		6	8		
	8	2		9				
2	5		9			1	4	
	9			3			6	
	3	6			7		5	9
				1		4	2	
		4	2		9	6		

2 2 1

	7			4		8		1
5			9	6			4	
9			3			1		4
	8		4	9	6		7	
2		4			7			6
	5			2	9			3
4		8		7			2	

2 2 2

				4		7		
		1	5			9		8
7			6	8				
1			9		5	8		
8		6				3		7
		4	8		7			9
				9	8			3
5		8			2	6		
		9		5				

5	3	1						
5	3	1						
		7	6	4	2		1	
		2				7	8	9
	6		8					
			1		5			
					6		2	
1	5	8				6		
	9		4	5	8	2		
						5	7	8

						3	1	5
			4	2	6			
7	8	9			1			
2				9				3
		7				5		
9				7				2
			5			2	4	9
			7	3	4			
4	5	8						

225

		8			6			7
		9					4	1
		7		1				3
	2	5		6			3	
	6		1		8		9	
	4			9		5	7	
1				2		6		
5	7					3		
3			6			7		

226

		7	8					3
	3					4	5	6
					3			9
			1		8		9	4
		6				8		
2	4		5		7			
4			7					
5	8	9					3	
7					5	9		

6				3	8		5	
8					9		1	7
		3		1				
							9	5
		1				6		
5	4							
				6		7		
2	5		7					8
	6		1	8				3

	3		6	4	1			8
2	7				8			
	4							6
7				5				
6		3				1		4
				3				5
1							8	
			8				6	7
5			7	6	4		1	

			5	9	4			
		4	8	3			1	
8		9						
		2	3				9	
1		5				8		2
	9				7	3		
						2		7
	4			7	9	6		
			6	5	3			

	5							
	8	3			9		5	
	7				5	4		8
7					1	3		
			6	4	3			
		8	7					5
6		2	4				3	
	1		2			5	6	
							8	

Puzzle 231

5	3		8		9		4	
			6	3		8	1	
		2					5	
7			9	4				
		6				9		
				8	6			5
	1					7		
	7	5		6	2			
	2		1		8		9	3

Puzzle 232

9		8			4			
					3	5	9	8
			1		8	4		
8	2	6						5
7						6	8	3
		5	8		7			
1	7	9	2					
			9			3		2

						1	3	8
			2	1	4	5		
9	1	7	5					
					2		4	
8		1				3		6
	9		8					
					6	2	1	3
		5	3	2	1			
1	2	3						

		5			8			1
		3			6		5	2
7		9						3
	1	4					3	
	6		1		3		2	
	7					9	1	
8						2		4
2	9		6			1		
4			2			3		

2 3 5

					5	4	7	3
			9	2	3		6	
5	6	3	7					
8								2
		5				9		
4								8
					7	2	3	4
	7		2	3	4			
2	3	4	6					

2 3 6

		4		5				2
	6	8						3
1		5	7					4
	4				3		2	
	1	9				6	3	
	2		8				4	
4					5	2		9
7						3	1	
6				2		4		

Puzzle 237

6	7	2						
		1	2	5	3			
			9			1	2	4
2	3				9			
	8						6	
			6				7	2
3	4	5			7			
			3	4	5	7		
						3	4	5

Puzzle 238

6			3			5		
1				9		4		8
7				8		3		
	1					8	5	
	3		7		2		4	
	5	6					3	
		2		3				5
3		8		1				4
		1			6			3

239

	8			5	7		3	
2	9							
	5		8					
1			3			7		
4			6		8			2
		5			9			3
					6		9	
							8	4
	4		9	3			7	

240

1						3	7	
4	2				3			
		3					6	1
		1	4			5		
3				5				8
		5			6	1		
8	1					7		
			7				8	2
	3	4						9

241

9		4				1		
	8		3			4	7	2
		7	5					
			6				3	
			9	5	7			
	6				4			
					5	3		
3	1	5			6		2	
		6				8		1

242

		3	8					
			3			2		7
	6	5						8
	4		6					2
	5		9	4	1		7	
1					8		6	
9						5	3	
5		2			4			
					3	1		

	5			9			2	
			4					9
2		3	5			4		
		7				3	5	
	2	5	8		9	6	4	
	6	4				2		
		6			8	9		5
7					1			
	8			6			7	

	9		1			2	3	
6						5		4
		2	5					
			2	5		7	8	
2		7				4		3
	8	3		9	7			
					1	8		
8		1						2
	3	9			2		6	

			6					
1	6	8		7	9			
	5						9	
7	9		3		6	5		
5			8		7			1
		6	4		5		3	9
	4						7	
			5	6		9	8	3
					2			

4	1			6	8			
								4
				7		8	6	5
		2						3
		5	9		4	6		
1						2		
8	4	9		5				
2								
			8	3			4	2

9	3					2	4	5
2				8			7	
7				4	3			
	2			6	8			
				7				
			9	3			5	
		5	1					8
	6			9				7
8	9	2					6	3

7		4						5
		6	5	4			2	
		1		8		7	3	
9			7					
				5				
					4			6
	3	8		2		9		
	2			9	6	3		
6						1		2

Puzzle 249:

7				6	9	8		
		6		4				
		2			3	9	7	
6							1	3
	4						2	
2	5							8
	2	8	3			1		
				8		7		
		4	1	5				9

Puzzle 250:

2	4			6		1		
3	1		9					
				5				
7			3	4	9	2		
		9				7		
		8	2	1	7			5
				3				
					1		4	8
		3		9			7	1

6	2			3		8		
3				9				
	4	9	5	7				
		3				5		
7		6		8		9		1
		4				3		
			6	4		2	3	
			2					5
		2		5			6	7

8	5			1			3	
	6				3	1		
3				8		5		
			4	3			1	2
			1		2			
2	4			5	6			
		9		6				5
		5	3				2	
	2			7			9	6

8							4	7
	9		8	3			1	
					2			8
						5	9	
7			9		6			4
	6	5						
5			2					
	1			4	3		7	
2	8							9

		3		6	8		5	
	9	2		7			3	
				2		4		
5					2			7
		4				9		
6			8					1
		8		1				
	3			8		6	9	
	6		3	9		8		

	2					9		7
				1			2	8
8					6			
	9	3	2			7		
		4	1		3	5		
		5			7	1	8	
			3					6
5	7			8				
3		2					7	

1				2				
2			4		9		1	
3				5		6	4	2
4						8	9	
	1						7	
	2	9						3
9	3	8		1				6
	4		2		5			9
				6				1

257

							5	
		1						
4	5	6	7				3	1
2				4	5	6	7	
		5	8		3	9		
	3	4	2	7				5
3	9				2	7	6	4
						5		
	4							

258

1	7	2		3		4		5
8			7					
5			4		9		2	
4	2							
			3		8			
							7	3
	9		2		1			4
					3			9
3		7		6		5	8	2

1					7	6		8
			3			7		
2			8			3		5
				2	6		3	
3								1
	4		9	3				
4		8			2			9
		7			5			
5		6	7					2

5		4		3		2		1
1					5			
6	9		4				5	
	4	6						9
9						8	1	
	1				6		4	7
			8					5
7		3		4		1		2

Puzzle 261

5		9					6	2
8							9	
4						3		7
			7		9		2	
3			2		1			5
	2		3		8			
2		5						6
	9							8
1	4					5		9

Puzzle 262

3				8				7
1		2		3	9	4		5
							6	3
	2					3		
		8		5		2		
		3					4	
5	7							
2		6	9	4		7		8
9				7				2

6				4	2		7	
5		4		3		2		1
							3	
	1					8		
			4	2	5			
		7					4	
	2							
1		3		7		6		2
	7		2	9				4

	5		6				4	
	7		1	2				6
	4	1					7	
			9			1		
	3	6				5	9	
		5			2			
	2					8	3	
9				7	8		1	
	1				9		6	

265

			1					
4	9			5	6			
1		2		3		4		5
8								6
	4		3		9		8	
9								3
2		7		9		8		1
			6	1			5	4
					2			

266

		1	3			7		
	5						3	
		2	8			1	4	9
	4		2		5	9		
		3				6		
		8	9		4		2	
1	8	4			3	5		
	6						7	
		5			8	4		

267

	9			8			7	
	6					8		
5		4		3		2		1
			3	6		1		
			9		5			
		3		7	2			
8		6		2		9		5
		9					6	
	1			5			4	

268

		5				1		
				7	3			2
	3	4	1	6		8	9	
		9					8	1
		3				5		
1	2					3		
	6	2		3	9	7	1	
7			4	1				
		1				9		

	5				4			
				8				2
8		1				6		
1		2	9	3		4		5
		5		2		9		
9		3		5	7	2		8
		7				3		6
2				1				
			6				4	

9	4			6		5		
			7					
		7	3	1		9		
7								6
1		2		3		4		5
8								7
		6		4	1	2		
				3				
		9		8			5	1

			3	1				6
9						3		
3	8			2				1
	3						4	5
			2	3	4			
2	9						7	
6				4			5	8
		3						7
4				5	7			

3		2		7	6	5	4	
		8						
	7			1		2		
	4		8					
			5	3	2			
					9		6	
		4		5			7	
						6		
	5	6	1	8		3		2

Puzzle 273

		8	4		3	9	7	
		9			7	4	6	
4			9			1		
	2			4				7
6				3			5	
		2			1			6
	5	6	8			7		
	9	1	7		2	5		

Puzzle 274

			6				7	
				8	7	5	9	2
			9	2	3			
	2	1				7		
	4						8	
		5				4	1	
			2	7	4			
6	7	4	3	9				
	1				6			

		1			5			
	8						3	
	7	5		8			4	9
			7					
3			4	1	6			7
					9			
5	1			4		3	2	
	4						5	
			2			6		

					1	8	9	5
		8					6	
			6				2	1
		5	8		2		1	4
7	3		1		9	6		
2	4				7			
	5					2		
6	7	9	4					

7				4		1	5	
2			8					
	1		2	6				8
8	9				7	2		
	3						7	
		7	6				8	3
9				2	3		1	
					8			9
	7	8		9				4

	9		2		7			
		7	4				6	2
	5				9			4
	8						7	1
		2				5		
1	7						4	
8			1				2	
5	6				4	3		
			3		5		1	

Puzzle 279

	7			8	3	5	4		
		5	1				8		
		8					6		
				2		3		6	8
				6		9			
	1	3		4		8			
			5					1	
			8				2	9	
			2	9	6	1			4

Puzzle 280

4						2		8
	2			9	5			
8	3		6		4	1		
			3					5
1	8						4	3
2					6			
		2	5		3		8	4
			2	4			7	
3		6						2

2								
		8	9			5		
5					2			1
		1	2	6		3		4
	3			5			9	
9		2		7	1	6		
3			5					6
		6			8	4		
								8

		1			7	8		9
		9	8				1	
				1	4			
				9		2		8
9	6		7		8		5	4
8		5		2				
			2	7				
	1				9	3		
2		3	6			9		

283

		6						2
1	4	5			7			
	2			6	8	5	4	
8				9		6		
				5				
		2		3				7
	5	1	2	7			9	
			9			1	7	6
9						3		

284

			1	8			4	7
4		1						
			5				3	
	4		8	6		7		
6		7		9		5		3
		5		7	1		6	
	5				8			
						8		2
3	8			4	7			

		5						
3	1			6	2			5
			7		5	4	3	
2			5	4				
		8		9		5		
				8	7			1
	9	6	8		4			
8			1	7			6	2
					1			

							2	
5			9		2			
1				8		9		
	7		2	1			4	8
		6				1		
2	4			3	6		7	
		8		2				7
			4		1			5
	6							

287

				3	1			
	8	5						
		9			7	4	6	
	2				6			
1	7			8			9	2
			2				8	
	9	7	4			6		
						9	2	
			1	7				

288

1		6					9	4
	9		7	6				
4		3		9				
			4		2	7		
8								2
		2	6		3			
				5		6		7
				3	7		5	
7	5					2		1

289

	8	3	5					
4	7						6	
	5				4		3	2
	1				9			
		5	3		8	1		
			4				8	
5	4		6				1	
	9						2	4
					7	3	5	

290

		7			1			
		5		4	2			
	4				8		1	5
6		2				8	7	
	5	3				6		1
9	8		7				6	
			9	3		7		
			8			2		

	9				2		6	
3		5					7	
6				3				4
2	1		6		9			
			1		5		9	3
4				8				6
	3					4		7
	8		4				5	

		1	8	2		6		
	8				9	4		
9						3	2	
7			2				1	
			1		3			
	3				4			7
	1	3						6
		5	3				8	
		6		9	2	1		

		4	7					5
			4					
2	7	3				9		
5					1			7
6		9				2		8
3			9					1
		6				3	8	2
					6			
8					4	6		

		2	5				7	
	7			2	9			
4						1		
	5	7		1		8		
	2			3			9	
		6		8		7	4	
		5						9
			2	5			6	
	3				4	5		

295

					9		3	1
9					6			8
5				2		7		
			6			1	4	
	5	2		1				
		4	7					5
8			1					6
3	1		4					

296

	7		5					
8				7	9		5	
4	3			2			7	8
					1			
6			8		2			9
			6					
7	1			5			9	6
	8		9	6				2
					3		4	

3			9					6
5				8	4		2	3
		5		4			7	
	4	9		3		6	1	
	2			6		5		
4	6		8	9				5
2					1			8

	8	9					2	
	2	4						9
		7	9		8			
		1		3	4			
	9			6			4	
			2	5		1		
			6		7	9		
2						4	5	
	1					3	8	

299

			5					
	5		9	1	2			3
						1	6	5
	3			9			5	8
		5				2		
1	2			8			4	
5	8	6						
9			1	5	3		8	
					7			

300

1		2		4	8			5
					7	1		
3			9				6	
		4				2		1
2		7				4		
	4				9			3
		3	7					
9			6	5		7		8

1

1	2	3	4	5	6	7	8	9
7	5	4	8	3	9	6	2	1
8	6	9	1	2	7	4	3	5
9	3	7	5	1	8	2	6	4
2	8	5	7	6	4	1	9	3
6	4	1	3	9	2	8	5	7
5	7	8	6	4	3	9	1	2
3	9	6	2	7	1	5	4	8
4	1	2	9	8	5	3	7	6

2

3	7	8	5	4	6	9	1	2
9	2	1	3	7	8	4	5	6
6	4	5	9	2	1	7	8	3
1	5	7	8	9	3	6	2	4
2	6	3	7	1	4	8	9	5
4	8	9	2	6	5	1	3	7
8	1	4	6	5	2	3	7	9
5	9	6	1	3	7	2	4	8
7	3	2	4	8	9	5	6	1

3

3	6	9	7	8	2	5	4	1
1	2	5	4	9	3	6	7	8
8	4	7	5	1	6	2	3	9
6	5	2	3	4	9	8	1	7
9	3	1	6	7	8	4	5	2
7	8	4	2	5	1	9	6	3
5	9	6	8	3	7	1	2	4
2	7	8	1	6	4	3	9	5
4	1	3	9	2	5	7	8	6

4

1	9	8	3	6	7	2	4	5
4	7	5	2	8	9	6	1	3
3	2	6	5	4	1	8	9	7
5	3	1	7	2	8	4	6	9
7	8	4	6	9	3	5	2	1
9	6	2	4	1	5	7	3	8
8	4	3	9	7	2	1	5	6
6	5	7	1	3	4	9	8	2
2	1	9	8	5	6	3	7	4

5

6	4	3	1	7	2	9	8	5
2	7	1	9	8	5	3	6	4
9	8	5	3	4	6	2	7	1
5	9	2	4	3	8	7	1	6
1	3	4	7	6	9	8	5	2
8	6	7	5	2	1	4	3	9
7	5	9	2	1	3	6	4	8
4	2	8	6	5	7	1	9	3
3	1	6	8	9	4	5	2	7

6

3	7	9	2	1	6	5	4	8
6	2	8	5	9	4	7	1	3
5	4	1	3	8	7	2	6	9
1	8	5	7	2	3	6	9	4
9	3	2	4	6	1	8	7	5
4	6	7	8	5	9	1	3	2
8	9	4	6	7	2	3	5	1
7	5	3	1	4	8	9	2	6
2	1	6	9	3	5	4	8	7

7

3	2	7	8	9	4	6	1	5
5	6	1	2	7	3	8	9	4
9	8	4	6	1	5	7	3	2
7	1	2	4	6	9	3	5	8
4	3	5	1	2	8	9	6	7
6	9	8	5	3	7	4	2	1
2	4	3	7	5	6	1	8	9
8	5	9	3	4	1	2	7	6
1	7	6	9	8	2	5	4	3

8

5	9	6	8	4	1	2	7	3
3	4	2	7	5	6	1	8	9
7	8	1	9	2	3	5	6	4
9	1	8	6	3	2	7	4	5
6	7	3	4	9	5	8	1	2
2	5	4	1	8	7	9	3	6
8	3	9	5	7	4	6	2	1
1	2	5	3	6	8	4	9	7
4	6	7	2	1	9	3	5	8

9

9	4	6	2	8	1	7	3	5
1	5	8	9	3	7	2	4	6
2	7	3	4	5	6	9	8	1
6	2	1	8	4	9	3	5	7
7	3	9	6	1	5	8	2	4
4	8	5	7	2	3	1	6	9
3	9	2	5	7	4	6	1	8
8	6	4	1	9	2	5	7	3
5	1	7	3	6	8	4	9	2

10

7	9	2	5	4	3	8	6	1
8	1	4	2	6	9	5	3	7
3	5	6	1	7	8	4	9	2
5	4	9	8	1	6	2	7	3
2	3	1	4	5	7	9	8	6
6	7	8	9	3	2	1	4	5
4	6	5	7	8	1	3	2	9
9	8	3	6	2	5	7	1	4
1	2	7	3	9	4	6	5	8

11

4	8	6	2	5	1	3	7	9
7	5	9	4	8	3	6	2	1
2	1	3	9	6	7	4	8	5
9	4	5	3	7	2	1	6	8
3	2	7	8	1	6	9	5	4
8	6	1	5	9	4	7	3	2
6	3	4	1	2	5	8	9	7
5	7	8	6	4	9	2	1	3
1	9	2	7	3	8	5	4	6

12

2	6	3	4	8	5	9	7	1
7	1	5	9	3	6	4	2	8
9	4	8	2	1	7	6	5	3
5	7	9	1	6	3	8	4	2
1	3	2	7	4	8	5	6	9
4	8	6	5	2	9	3	1	7
6	5	7	3	9	1	2	8	4
8	9	4	6	7	2	1	3	5
3	2	1	8	5	4	7	9	6

13

4	7	8	2	5	6	1	9	3
1	6	3	9	7	8	5	4	2
9	2	5	4	3	1	7	6	8
3	4	7	6	2	5	9	8	1
2	5	6	8	1	9	3	7	4
8	1	9	3	4	7	6	2	5
7	8	2	1	6	3	4	5	9
6	9	1	5	8	4	2	3	7
5	3	4	7	9	2	8	1	6

14

1	8	9	4	2	6	3	7	5
2	4	7	1	5	3	6	9	8
6	3	5	7	8	9	4	1	2
3	9	8	5	4	2	1	6	7
7	1	6	3	9	8	5	2	4
4	5	2	6	7	1	9	8	3
8	6	3	2	1	5	7	4	9
9	7	1	8	3	4	2	5	6
5	2	4	9	6	7	8	3	1

15

3	7	4	6	8	9	1	5	2
5	1	6	2	3	4	7	8	9
8	2	9	7	5	1	6	4	3
2	5	8	3	1	7	9	6	4
4	9	1	5	6	8	3	2	7
6	3	7	9	4	2	8	1	5
9	4	5	8	7	6	2	3	1
1	8	2	4	9	3	5	7	6
7	6	3	1	2	5	4	9	8

16

3	9	5	1	7	2	8	4	6
4	2	7	8	3	6	5	9	1
8	1	6	4	5	9	7	3	2
5	4	8	6	2	3	9	1	7
2	7	1	5	9	8	3	6	4
9	6	3	7	1	4	2	5	8
1	3	2	9	6	7	4	8	5
6	8	9	2	4	5	1	7	3
7	5	4	3	8	1	6	2	9

17

9	6	1	5	8	2	4	7	3
5	3	2	1	4	7	8	9	6
4	7	8	3	9	6	1	2	5
1	4	9	6	2	5	7	3	8
2	8	6	7	3	4	5	1	9
7	5	3	8	1	9	6	4	2
6	2	7	4	5	3	9	8	1
3	1	5	9	7	8	2	6	4
8	9	4	2	6	1	3	5	7

18

8	7	6	3	4	2	5	1	9
1	3	4	9	8	5	6	2	7
5	9	2	6	7	1	8	4	3
7	8	5	2	9	3	1	6	4
3	2	1	5	6	4	9	7	8
4	6	9	8	1	7	3	5	2
2	1	3	4	5	8	7	9	6
9	4	7	1	3	6	2	8	5
6	5	8	7	2	9	4	3	1

19

3	8	4	7	9	2	6	1	5
7	2	5	3	1	6	8	9	4
9	6	1	8	4	5	2	3	7
2	3	6	9	8	4	7	5	1
5	7	9	2	3	1	4	8	6
1	4	8	6	5	7	9	2	3
6	1	2	5	7	8	3	4	9
4	9	7	1	2	3	5	6	8
8	5	3	4	6	9	1	7	2

20

6	9	1	2	5	3	4	7	8
7	2	4	9	8	1	3	6	5
5	8	3	7	6	4	2	9	1
4	7	9	1	2	6	5	8	3
1	5	8	4	3	9	7	2	6
3	6	2	5	7	8	1	4	9
9	1	5	6	4	7	8	3	2
8	4	6	3	1	2	9	5	7
2	3	7	8	9	5	6	1	4

21

9	6	1	5	3	8	4	7	2
7	3	8	4	1	2	6	9	5
2	5	4	7	9	6	8	3	1
3	7	6	1	4	5	2	8	9
1	4	2	6	8	9	7	5	3
5	8	9	2	7	3	1	6	4
8	1	5	9	6	4	3	2	7
4	2	3	8	5	7	9	1	6
6	9	7	3	2	1	5	4	8

22

8	4	3	7	1	9	6	2	5
7	1	2	3	6	5	8	9	4
6	9	5	4	2	8	1	3	7
5	7	1	8	9	2	4	6	3
9	2	8	6	3	4	5	7	1
4	3	6	5	7	1	2	8	9
1	8	9	2	4	7	3	5	6
3	5	7	1	8	6	9	4	2
2	6	4	9	5	3	7	1	8

23

6	5	1	9	7	3	8	4	2
7	3	9	8	2	4	1	5	6
4	2	8	6	5	1	3	9	7
3	8	7	4	9	5	6	2	1
1	9	2	7	3	6	4	8	5
5	4	6	1	8	2	9	7	3
8	1	5	3	4	7	2	6	9
2	6	4	5	1	9	7	3	8
9	7	3	2	6	8	5	1	4

24

3	7	8	1	5	4	9	6	2
6	1	2	9	7	3	4	5	8
4	9	5	2	6	8	7	1	3
1	6	3	8	4	5	2	7	9
5	8	9	3	2	7	6	4	1
7	2	4	6	9	1	8	3	5
8	5	7	4	3	9	1	2	6
2	3	1	7	8	6	5	9	4
9	4	6	5	1	2	3	8	7

25

8	2	6	9	5	1	3	7	4
3	1	5	4	2	7	9	6	8
9	4	7	3	8	6	5	1	2
1	7	2	6	3	8	4	9	5
5	3	4	2	7	9	1	8	6
6	8	9	1	4	5	7	2	3
4	5	1	7	6	2	8	3	9
2	9	8	5	1	3	6	4	7
7	6	3	8	9	4	2	5	1

26

6	3	5	1	9	8	4	7	2
8	2	7	6	5	4	3	1	9
9	1	4	3	2	7	5	8	6
2	4	8	7	3	5	9	6	1
5	9	3	8	6	1	2	4	7
1	7	6	9	4	2	8	3	5
3	6	2	4	7	9	1	5	8
4	8	9	5	1	6	7	2	3
7	5	1	2	8	3	6	9	4

27

3	6	7	5	2	1	9	4	8
8	1	2	7	4	9	5	3	6
5	9	4	8	3	6	2	7	1
9	2	1	6	8	7	3	5	4
6	4	5	9	1	3	8	2	7
7	8	3	2	5	4	1	6	9
2	3	9	4	6	8	7	1	5
4	5	8	1	7	2	6	9	3
1	7	6	3	9	5	4	8	2

28

3	9	1	4	7	2	8	5	6
7	5	8	9	3	6	1	4	2
6	4	2	8	5	1	3	7	9
9	8	7	1	6	4	5	2	3
4	1	3	2	9	5	6	8	7
5	2	6	7	8	3	4	9	1
2	7	4	3	1	8	9	6	5
1	6	9	5	4	7	2	3	8
8	3	5	6	2	9	7	1	4

29

5	6	9	7	2	4	1	3	8
7	4	3	8	5	1	6	2	9
1	8	2	9	3	6	4	7	5
8	2	4	5	6	7	9	1	3
3	9	1	4	8	2	5	6	7
6	7	5	1	9	3	2	8	4
9	5	6	2	7	8	3	4	1
2	1	8	3	4	5	7	9	6
4	3	7	6	1	9	8	5	2

30

7	5	6	9	3	1	2	4	8
2	9	8	7	4	5	3	1	6
3	4	1	8	6	2	7	9	5
8	7	5	4	2	9	1	6	3
1	3	4	6	8	7	9	5	2
9	6	2	5	1	3	4	8	7
5	2	3	1	9	8	6	7	4
4	8	9	3	7	6	5	2	1
6	1	7	2	5	4	8	3	9

31

8	6	2	4	1	9	3	7	5
5	7	4	8	3	6	2	9	1
9	1	3	2	5	7	8	6	4
6	3	9	1	2	5	4	8	7
7	4	5	6	9	8	1	2	3
1	2	8	7	4	3	6	5	9
2	5	7	3	6	4	9	1	8
3	8	1	9	7	2	5	4	6
4	9	6	5	8	1	7	3	2

32

3	1	8	9	2	5	4	6	7
7	9	6	4	3	8	1	5	2
4	2	5	1	7	6	3	9	8
1	8	9	5	4	2	7	3	6
2	3	4	7	6	1	9	8	5
5	6	7	3	8	9	2	4	1
8	4	1	2	5	3	6	7	9
6	7	2	8	9	4	5	1	3
9	5	3	6	1	7	8	2	4

33

4	6	7	5	9	2	8	3	1
1	9	2	8	3	6	4	7	5
8	3	5	7	4	1	6	9	2
2	1	9	4	5	3	7	6	8
5	7	8	1	6	9	2	4	3
3	4	6	2	8	7	5	1	9
7	2	4	9	1	8	3	5	6
9	5	3	6	2	4	1	8	7
6	8	1	3	7	5	9	2	4

34

5	9	2	6	3	8	7	1	4
7	6	3	1	4	9	8	5	2
4	1	8	7	5	2	9	6	3
9	7	5	8	2	6	3	4	1
3	8	1	5	9	4	6	2	7
6	2	4	3	1	7	5	9	8
2	5	7	4	6	3	1	8	9
8	4	6	9	7	1	2	3	5
1	3	9	2	8	5	4	7	6

35

5	6	4	8	3	7	2	9	1
7	2	8	6	1	9	5	4	3
9	3	1	5	2	4	6	8	7
4	8	7	1	9	5	3	6	2
3	9	5	2	6	8	7	1	4
6	1	2	7	4	3	9	5	8
8	5	6	3	7	1	4	2	9
2	7	9	4	8	6	1	3	5
1	4	3	9	5	2	8	7	6

36

1	7	4	2	6	5	8	3	9
6	8	9	4	3	1	2	5	7
2	3	5	9	7	8	1	6	4
8	5	2	3	9	6	7	4	1
3	4	6	1	8	7	9	2	5
7	9	1	5	2	4	6	8	3
4	1	7	6	5	2	3	9	8
9	6	8	7	4	3	5	1	2
5	2	3	8	1	9	4	7	6

37

1	8	2	9	3	7	4	6	5
5	6	4	2	8	1	7	3	9
9	7	3	5	4	6	1	8	2
7	1	9	4	5	3	6	2	8
3	5	6	1	2	8	9	4	7
4	2	8	6	7	9	3	5	1
8	3	5	7	9	4	2	1	6
2	9	1	3	6	5	8	7	4
6	4	7	8	1	2	5	9	3

38

9	3	4	8	5	6	2	7	1
2	8	5	1	4	7	3	6	9
7	1	6	9	3	2	4	8	5
1	4	7	3	2	8	9	5	6
5	9	3	4	6	1	7	2	8
8	6	2	5	7	9	1	3	4
4	2	8	6	1	3	5	9	7
3	5	9	7	8	4	6	1	2
6	7	1	2	9	5	8	4	3

39

1	2	3	4	9	6	8	7	5
9	8	5	7	1	2	3	4	6
6	7	4	8	5	3	9	2	1
3	9	1	2	4	8	6	5	7
4	5	7	3	6	1	2	8	9
2	6	8	5	7	9	1	3	4
5	1	2	6	8	4	7	9	3
7	3	9	1	2	5	4	6	8
8	4	6	9	3	7	5	1	2

40

3	2	6	7	1	5	9	4	8
9	8	7	6	2	4	5	3	1
1	5	4	3	9	8	7	6	2
7	1	5	8	3	9	6	2	4
2	3	9	4	6	1	8	7	5
6	4	8	2	5	7	1	9	3
8	6	2	5	7	3	4	1	9
4	9	3	1	8	6	2	5	7
5	7	1	9	4	2	3	8	6

4/1

2	9	4	3	8	7	5	1	6
1	8	3	6	5	9	2	4	7
6	7	5	4	1	2	9	8	3
5	6	2	1	4	8	3	7	9
7	1	9	5	2	3	4	6	8
4	3	8	7	9	6	1	5	2
8	5	7	2	3	1	6	9	4
3	4	6	9	7	5	8	2	1
9	2	1	8	6	4	7	3	5

4/2

2	3	9	7	8	5	1	4	6
1	8	6	4	2	9	5	3	7
7	4	5	6	1	3	2	8	9
9	5	2	3	7	6	8	1	4
3	1	4	5	9	8	7	6	2
6	7	8	2	4	1	9	5	3
4	2	1	8	6	7	3	9	5
5	9	7	1	3	4	6	2	8
8	6	3	9	5	2	4	7	1

4/3

6	9	1	2	8	7	5	4	3
4	3	2	6	9	5	7	8	1
7	8	5	4	1	3	2	9	6
8	5	3	1	2	4	9	6	7
9	6	7	5	3	8	1	2	4
2	1	4	9	7	6	3	5	8
3	4	9	8	5	1	6	7	2
5	7	8	3	6	2	4	1	9
1	2	6	7	4	9	8	3	5

4/4

7	2	5	3	6	1	9	8	4
8	1	4	5	2	9	7	6	3
6	3	9	4	8	7	1	2	5
1	8	6	7	9	4	3	5	2
5	4	3	8	1	2	6	9	7
9	7	2	6	3	5	8	4	1
3	6	1	2	5	8	4	7	9
4	5	8	9	7	3	2	1	6
2	9	7	1	4	6	5	3	8

4/5

9	2	8	1	7	6	3	4	5
1	6	5	8	4	3	2	9	7
7	3	4	9	2	5	8	1	6
8	5	2	4	3	9	7	6	1
3	7	9	2	6	1	5	8	4
6	4	1	5	8	7	9	3	2
4	1	3	7	9	2	6	5	8
2	8	6	3	5	4	1	7	9
5	9	7	6	1	8	4	2	3

4/6

2	7	6	3	5	8	1	9	4
5	8	1	2	4	9	7	3	6
4	3	9	6	1	7	2	8	5
8	5	3	9	6	2	4	1	7
9	2	4	8	7	1	5	6	3
6	1	7	4	3	5	8	2	9
7	4	2	1	9	6	3	5	8
1	9	5	7	8	3	6	4	2
3	6	8	5	2	4	9	7	1

4/7

5	8	9	2	1	6	4	3	7
2	1	4	8	7	3	5	9	6
6	3	7	5	9	4	2	1	8
8	9	1	3	2	7	6	5	4
4	2	5	6	8	1	9	7	3
3	7	6	9	4	5	1	8	2
7	6	8	4	5	9	3	2	1
1	5	3	7	6	2	8	4	9
9	4	2	1	3	8	7	6	5

4/8

8	9	6	1	2	3	4	5	7
5	4	3	8	6	7	1	2	9
7	1	2	9	5	4	8	6	3
1	3	8	6	4	2	9	7	5
6	7	9	5	3	1	2	8	4
2	5	4	7	9	8	3	1	6
3	6	7	2	1	9	5	4	8
4	8	1	3	7	5	6	9	2
9	2	5	4	8	6	7	3	1

49

6	8	2	9	7	1	3	4	5
7	1	5	3	2	4	8	9	6
4	9	3	8	5	6	7	2	1
8	2	6	7	9	5	4	1	3
5	7	1	4	6	3	2	8	9
9	3	4	1	8	2	5	6	7
1	4	7	2	3	9	6	5	8
2	5	8	6	1	7	9	3	4
3	6	9	5	4	8	1	7	2

50

6	5	8	3	1	9	2	7	4
4	7	9	2	6	8	3	1	5
2	3	1	7	4	5	9	8	6
9	2	3	5	7	6	1	4	8
1	6	5	8	2	4	7	3	9
8	4	7	1	9	3	6	5	2
7	9	4	6	8	1	5	2	3
5	1	6	4	3	2	8	9	7
3	8	2	9	5	7	4	6	1

51

2	4	6	7	9	8	3	5	1
1	3	5	4	6	2	9	8	7
7	9	8	5	3	1	4	2	6
6	7	3	9	1	5	2	4	8
5	2	9	8	7	4	1	6	3
8	1	4	3	2	6	7	9	5
9	8	1	6	4	7	5	3	2
3	5	2	1	8	9	6	7	4
4	6	7	2	5	3	8	1	9

52

3	8	2	5	9	6	1	4	7
1	9	6	7	8	4	3	2	5
5	7	4	2	1	3	9	8	6
9	4	5	6	3	7	2	1	8
7	2	3	1	5	8	6	9	4
8	6	1	9	4	2	7	5	3
6	5	7	8	2	1	4	3	9
2	3	8	4	6	9	5	7	1
4	1	9	3	7	5	8	6	2

53

1	3	5	9	7	8	2	4	6
8	9	7	2	4	6	5	1	3
2	4	6	3	1	5	9	8	7
6	8	4	7	9	3	1	2	5
5	1	3	6	2	4	8	7	9
7	2	9	8	5	1	6	3	4
4	6	8	1	3	9	7	5	2
9	5	2	4	8	7	3	6	1
3	7	1	5	6	2	4	9	8

54

2	3	6	5	9	1	4	7	8
1	9	5	8	4	7	3	6	2
8	4	7	3	2	6	5	9	1
9	5	2	1	3	8	6	4	7
6	1	3	4	7	9	8	2	5
4	7	8	2	6	5	9	1	3
3	2	1	6	5	4	7	8	9
5	6	9	7	8	2	1	3	4
7	8	4	9	1	3	2	5	6

55

7	5	1	2	3	6	8	4	9
2	4	3	5	9	8	7	6	1
6	8	9	4	7	1	5	3	2
8	9	6	7	5	4	2	1	3
3	2	4	1	8	9	6	5	7
5	1	7	6	2	3	4	9	8
1	3	2	8	6	5	9	7	4
9	6	8	3	4	7	1	2	5
4	7	5	9	1	2	3	8	6

56

9	8	7	6	5	4	3	1	2
3	5	4	7	1	2	6	9	8
6	1	2	9	8	3	7	4	5
5	2	9	4	7	6	1	8	3
7	3	1	5	2	8	9	6	4
8	4	6	1	3	9	2	5	7
2	9	5	3	4	1	8	7	6
4	6	8	2	9	7	5	3	1
1	7	3	8	6	5	4	2	9

5/7

8	4	2	7	9	5	3	6	1
3	6	1	2	8	4	5	7	9
5	7	9	3	1	6	8	4	2
1	3	7	6	2	8	4	9	5
4	2	5	1	3	9	6	8	7
6	9	8	5	4	7	2	1	3
7	8	4	9	5	3	1	2	6
9	1	3	4	6	2	7	5	8
2	5	6	8	7	1	9	3	4

5/8

4	1	9	5	8	7	6	2	3
7	8	5	3	6	2	4	1	9
6	3	2	4	9	1	7	5	8
9	5	8	6	4	3	2	7	1
1	2	6	8	7	5	3	9	4
3	4	7	2	1	9	5	8	6
5	6	3	1	2	8	9	4	7
8	9	4	7	5	6	1	3	2
2	7	1	9	3	4	8	6	5

5/9

8	4	9	3	5	6	1	7	2
3	6	1	2	4	7	5	9	8
7	2	5	9	8	1	6	3	4
9	1	8	6	3	5	4	2	7
2	3	7	4	1	9	8	5	6
4	5	6	8	7	2	3	1	9
6	7	3	1	2	8	9	4	5
5	9	4	7	6	3	2	8	1
1	8	2	5	9	4	7	6	3

6/0

2	3	9	8	1	7	5	4	6
4	5	1	6	3	2	8	7	9
6	7	8	9	4	5	2	1	3
8	9	4	7	2	6	1	3	5
3	6	7	5	8	1	9	2	4
5	1	2	4	9	3	6	8	7
7	4	5	2	6	8	3	9	1
9	8	3	1	5	4	7	6	2
1	2	6	3	7	9	4	5	8

6/1

1	4	9	2	3	5	8	6	7
2	5	8	6	1	7	4	9	3
3	7	6	8	9	4	2	5	1
9	2	5	3	4	1	7	8	6
6	3	1	7	8	9	5	2	4
7	8	4	5	2	6	3	1	9
5	9	7	4	6	8	1	3	2
8	6	3	1	7	2	9	4	5
4	1	2	9	5	3	6	7	8

6/2

9	2	4	3	5	6	7	8	1
7	3	8	9	1	4	2	6	5
5	1	6	7	2	8	3	4	9
3	7	2	8	9	5	4	1	6
1	8	5	4	6	2	9	3	7
6	4	9	1	3	7	5	2	8
2	9	3	5	8	1	6	7	4
8	5	7	6	4	3	1	9	2
4	6	1	2	7	9	8	5	3

6/3

1	8	2	3	5	4	9	7	6
3	9	4	8	7	6	5	2	1
5	6	7	2	9	1	3	4	8
7	5	8	4	6	9	2	1	3
9	1	6	5	3	2	7	8	4
2	4	3	7	1	8	6	9	5
8	3	5	9	4	7	1	6	2
6	2	9	1	8	5	4	3	7
4	7	1	6	2	3	8	5	9

6/4

9	7	5	3	1	4	8	2	6
1	8	3	2	9	6	5	7	4
2	4	6	7	5	8	3	9	1
8	3	9	1	4	7	6	5	2
4	5	7	6	8	2	9	1	3
6	1	2	5	3	9	7	4	8
7	9	1	8	2	3	4	6	5
3	2	4	9	6	5	1	8	7
5	6	8	4	7	1	2	3	9

65

6	3	4	8	2	7	5	1	9
5	1	7	6	9	3	2	4	8
9	2	8	4	1	5	3	7	6
3	9	5	1	6	2	4	8	7
1	8	6	5	7	4	9	3	2
7	4	2	3	8	9	6	5	1
4	7	1	2	5	6	8	9	3
2	5	9	7	3	8	1	6	4
8	6	3	9	4	1	7	2	5

66

2	3	5	4	9	7	8	1	6
6	1	9	5	8	2	7	3	4
8	4	7	1	3	6	2	5	9
4	2	1	7	6	5	3	9	8
9	8	6	2	4	3	1	7	5
5	7	3	9	1	8	4	6	2
1	9	2	3	5	4	6	8	7
7	5	8	6	2	1	9	4	3
3	6	4	8	7	9	5	2	1

67

2	6	8	9	1	4	5	3	7
4	7	1	3	5	8	9	2	6
5	9	3	2	6	7	4	1	8
8	1	7	4	3	6	2	5	9
3	4	6	5	9	2	7	8	1
9	5	2	7	8	1	3	6	4
7	8	5	6	4	3	1	9	2
6	3	4	1	2	9	8	7	5
1	2	9	8	7	5	6	4	3

68

2	5	4	9	3	7	8	1	6
6	1	3	2	4	8	9	7	5
9	8	7	1	6	5	2	3	4
4	3	9	8	5	1	6	2	7
8	7	5	4	2	6	1	9	3
1	2	6	7	9	3	5	4	8
3	4	8	6	1	9	7	5	2
7	9	2	5	8	4	3	6	1
5	6	1	3	7	2	4	8	9

69

3	4	2	9	7	1	8	6	5
8	6	7	3	2	5	1	9	4
1	5	9	4	8	6	7	2	3
7	3	1	8	6	4	2	5	9
9	2	4	1	5	3	6	7	8
6	8	5	2	9	7	3	4	1
4	7	8	5	1	2	9	3	6
2	9	3	6	4	8	5	1	7
5	1	6	7	3	9	4	8	2

70

8	4	2	9	5	6	3	7	1
7	9	6	8	1	3	5	2	4
5	1	3	2	7	4	9	6	8
6	7	5	3	9	1	4	8	2
4	3	8	7	2	5	1	9	6
1	2	9	4	6	8	7	3	5
9	6	7	5	4	2	8	1	3
2	8	4	1	3	9	6	5	7
3	5	1	6	8	7	2	4	9

71

1	2	3	9	8	7	6	5	4
9	8	7	4	5	6	1	2	3
4	6	5	1	2	3	7	8	9
8	5	9	6	7	1	3	4	2
3	7	4	2	9	5	8	1	6
2	1	6	3	4	8	5	9	7
5	9	1	7	6	2	4	3	8
6	4	8	5	3	9	2	7	1
7	3	2	8	1	4	9	6	5

72

1	2	3	9	8	4	7	5	6
4	5	6	3	2	7	8	9	1
7	8	9	1	5	6	3	2	4
3	6	5	7	1	8	2	4	9
8	9	7	2	4	5	6	1	3
2	1	4	6	9	3	5	8	7
5	7	2	4	6	1	9	3	8
6	4	8	5	3	9	1	7	2
9	3	1	8	7	2	4	6	5

7/3

1	2	3	4	8	9	6	5	7
6	5	4	7	3	1	9	2	8
9	8	7	5	2	6	3	4	1
8	4	1	6	5	3	7	9	2
2	7	5	8	9	4	1	6	3
3	9	6	1	7	2	4	8	5
5	1	9	2	4	7	8	3	6
4	6	2	3	1	8	5	7	9
7	3	8	9	6	5	2	1	4

7/4

3	6	9	7	5	2	4	1	8
5	8	2	3	4	1	6	9	7
1	4	7	9	6	8	2	3	5
7	1	5	4	2	3	8	6	9
8	2	3	1	9	6	7	5	4
4	9	6	5	8	7	3	2	1
2	5	8	6	7	9	1	4	3
6	3	4	8	1	5	9	7	2
9	7	1	2	3	4	5	8	6

7/5

2	9	3	1	6	5	8	4	7
1	4	5	2	8	7	3	6	9
7	6	8	9	4	3	2	5	1
4	8	7	5	2	1	9	3	6
3	2	9	6	7	4	1	8	5
6	5	1	3	9	8	7	2	4
5	1	4	8	3	9	6	7	2
9	3	2	7	5	6	4	1	8
8	7	6	4	1	2	5	9	3

7/6

5	6	1	7	2	8	3	4	9
8	3	9	1	4	6	2	7	5
4	2	7	5	3	9	1	8	6
2	1	8	4	5	3	9	6	7
6	4	5	2	9	7	8	1	3
9	7	3	8	6	1	4	5	2
3	5	6	9	1	4	7	2	8
7	9	4	6	8	2	5	3	1
1	8	2	3	7	5	6	9	4

7/7

7	5	6	8	2	3	1	4	9
9	3	1	7	6	4	8	2	5
8	4	2	9	1	5	6	3	7
2	8	9	4	5	6	7	1	3
4	7	3	2	9	1	5	6	8
1	6	5	3	7	8	4	9	2
5	2	8	1	4	9	3	7	6
6	1	7	5	3	2	9	8	4
3	9	4	6	8	7	2	5	1

7/8

5	8	2	1	7	3	9	4	6
7	3	9	2	6	4	5	1	8
1	6	4	8	9	5	7	3	2
9	2	5	6	3	7	4	8	1
6	1	3	5	4	8	2	9	7
4	7	8	9	1	2	3	6	5
8	4	1	7	5	9	6	2	3
2	9	7	3	8	6	1	5	4
3	5	6	4	2	1	8	7	9

7/9

1	2	3	8	9	7	4	5	6
5	7	9	4	3	6	2	8	1
6	4	8	5	2	1	3	7	9
8	1	5	7	6	2	9	3	4
2	3	4	1	8	9	5	6	7
9	6	7	3	5	4	8	1	2
3	9	2	6	1	5	7	4	8
7	8	1	2	4	3	6	9	5
4	5	6	9	7	8	1	2	3

8/0

1	4	3	7	9	6	5	8	2
5	8	6	4	2	1	3	7	9
2	9	7	3	5	8	4	6	1
9	1	2	5	7	3	6	4	8
6	3	5	8	1	4	9	2	7
8	7	4	2	6	9	1	3	5
3	2	1	9	4	7	8	5	6
7	6	8	1	3	5	2	9	4
4	5	9	6	8	2	7	1	3

8-1

5	2	4	7	9	8	3	6	1
3	7	9	4	1	6	5	2	8
6	8	1	5	2	3	9	4	7
7	6	5	1	8	9	2	3	4
1	4	3	6	5	2	7	8	9
8	9	2	3	7	4	1	5	6
9	1	8	2	6	5	4	7	3
2	3	7	8	4	1	6	9	5
4	5	6	9	3	7	8	1	2

8-2

1	9	8	7	4	5	6	3	2
6	5	2	1	9	3	8	4	7
3	7	4	2	6	8	5	1	9
8	6	5	3	1	7	2	9	4
9	4	7	6	5	2	3	8	1
2	1	3	4	8	9	7	6	5
4	3	6	5	7	1	9	2	8
5	8	1	9	2	6	4	7	3
7	2	9	8	3	4	1	5	6

8-3

6	8	5	2	1	7	3	9	4
2	1	9	4	6	3	5	7	8
3	7	4	9	5	8	6	1	2
9	5	3	6	4	2	1	8	7
1	2	6	8	7	5	9	4	3
8	4	7	3	9	1	2	6	5
5	6	8	7	3	9	4	2	1
4	3	2	1	8	6	7	5	9
7	9	1	5	2	4	8	3	6

8-4

5	6	4	2	7	3	8	1	9
1	3	2	8	4	9	7	6	5
8	7	9	5	6	1	4	2	3
3	4	5	9	8	6	2	7	1
2	8	7	4	1	5	9	3	6
9	1	6	3	2	7	5	8	4
7	9	1	6	5	2	3	4	8
6	5	8	7	3	4	1	9	2
4	2	3	1	9	8	6	5	7

8-5

1	7	6	3	9	4	8	2	5
8	2	5	7	6	1	9	3	4
9	4	3	5	2	8	1	6	7
7	1	8	4	3	9	6	5	2
4	6	2	8	5	7	3	9	1
5	3	9	2	1	6	4	7	8
3	5	1	9	8	2	7	4	6
6	9	4	1	7	5	2	8	3
2	8	7	6	4	3	5	1	9

8-6

8	2	9	6	7	5	3	1	4
1	3	6	9	4	8	5	7	2
7	4	5	1	2	3	6	9	8
6	8	1	2	9	4	7	5	3
5	9	2	3	6	7	8	4	1
4	7	3	5	8	1	9	2	6
9	1	8	4	5	6	2	3	7
3	5	7	8	1	2	4	6	9
2	6	4	7	3	9	1	8	5

8-7

6	8	3	4	5	9	2	1	7
1	5	9	7	8	2	4	6	3
7	2	4	1	6	3	8	9	5
2	1	7	3	4	5	6	8	9
3	6	8	2	9	1	5	7	4
4	9	5	6	7	8	1	3	2
8	4	1	5	3	7	9	2	6
9	7	6	8	2	4	3	5	1
5	3	2	9	1	6	7	4	8

8-8

4	5	7	8	2	1	9	3	6
3	2	6	5	9	7	4	1	8
9	1	8	3	6	4	2	7	5
7	6	3	4	8	9	1	5	2
1	9	2	7	3	5	6	8	4
5	8	4	2	1	6	7	9	3
2	3	9	6	7	8	5	4	1
8	7	5	1	4	2	3	6	9
6	4	1	9	5	3	8	2	7

6	2	9	1	7	5	4	3	8
7	3	8	2	9	4	5	6	1
5	1	4	3	8	6	7	2	9
8	5	2	7	4	1	3	9	6
3	4	6	9	5	2	8	1	7
9	7	1	8	6	3	2	4	5
1	6	3	5	2	7	9	8	4
2	9	5	4	1	8	6	7	3
4	8	7	6	3	9	1	5	2

3	9	7	5	2	1	6	4	8
2	1	4	3	6	8	5	9	7
6	8	5	9	4	7	1	2	3
1	2	3	8	7	9	4	6	5
8	7	9	4	5	6	2	3	1
4	5	6	1	3	2	7	8	9
9	3	2	7	1	4	8	5	6
7	6	8	2	9	5	3	1	4
5	4	1	6	8	3	9	7	2

7	3	2	6	8	4	5	1	9
8	9	4	5	3	1	6	7	2
1	5	6	2	7	9	3	8	4
9	4	8	1	2	3	7	6	5
5	1	7	9	4	6	8	2	3
2	6	3	8	5	7	4	9	1
4	8	1	7	9	5	2	3	6
6	7	5	3	1	2	9	4	8
3	2	9	4	6	8	1	5	7

3	2	7	6	5	9	8	1	4
1	8	6	2	7	4	9	3	5
5	4	9	8	1	3	2	6	7
6	1	8	9	3	7	5	4	2
7	3	5	1	4	2	6	9	8
4	9	2	5	8	6	3	7	1
9	6	1	4	2	5	7	8	3
8	5	3	7	9	1	4	2	6
2	7	4	3	6	8	1	5	9

6	2	1	3	5	4	9	8	7
8	7	4	6	9	2	1	3	5
3	9	5	1	7	8	2	4	6
2	1	9	8	4	6	5	7	3
4	5	6	9	3	7	8	2	1
7	3	8	5	2	1	4	6	9
9	4	2	7	6	5	3	1	8
1	6	3	2	8	9	7	5	4
5	8	7	4	1	3	6	9	2

5	1	4	3	9	6	2	8	7
8	7	9	5	1	2	4	6	3
6	2	3	4	7	8	5	9	1
7	5	8	2	6	1	9	3	4
9	4	2	8	3	5	1	7	6
3	6	1	9	4	7	8	2	5
4	8	6	1	2	3	7	5	9
1	3	5	7	8	9	6	4	2
2	9	7	6	5	4	3	1	8

5	4	7	6	1	2	8	9	3
9	3	8	4	5	7	2	1	6
6	2	1	3	8	9	7	4	5
4	1	9	8	7	6	5	3	2
8	6	3	1	2	5	9	7	4
7	5	2	9	4	3	1	6	8
3	8	4	2	9	1	6	5	7
1	7	6	5	3	8	4	2	9
2	9	5	7	6	4	3	8	1

5	6	7	9	4	8	3	2	1
2	3	4	6	5	1	8	9	7
9	8	1	2	3	7	6	4	5
8	5	6	4	7	3	2	1	9
3	1	2	5	9	6	4	7	8
7	4	9	8	1	2	5	6	3
6	7	8	1	2	5	9	3	4
1	9	5	3	6	4	7	8	2
4	2	3	7	8	9	1	5	6

97

7	6	8	9	2	5	1	3	4
2	9	3	8	1	4	5	7	6
1	4	5	6	3	7	2	8	9
8	5	1	2	4	9	3	6	7
4	7	6	1	5	3	8	9	2
9	3	2	7	6	8	4	5	1
5	1	7	4	8	6	9	2	3
3	2	9	5	7	1	6	4	8
6	8	4	3	9	2	7	1	5

98

9	3	2	1	7	8	5	4	6
6	4	7	5	2	9	8	1	3
5	8	1	6	4	3	2	9	7
7	9	6	8	1	2	4	3	5
3	5	4	9	6	7	1	2	8
1	2	8	3	5	4	6	7	9
8	6	3	4	9	1	7	5	2
2	1	9	7	8	5	3	6	4
4	7	5	2	3	6	9	8	1

99

2	3	8	6	7	1	4	5	9
5	9	6	4	8	2	1	3	7
7	4	1	9	5	3	6	2	8
6	7	9	5	1	4	2	8	3
1	5	3	2	9	8	7	6	4
4	8	2	3	6	7	5	9	1
8	1	5	7	2	9	3	4	6
3	2	7	8	4	6	9	1	5
9	6	4	1	3	5	8	7	2

100

8	5	4	2	6	3	9	7	1
7	1	6	4	8	9	2	3	5
2	3	9	1	5	7	6	8	4
9	7	5	6	2	1	3	4	8
1	2	3	7	4	8	5	6	9
4	6	8	9	3	5	1	2	7
3	4	7	5	1	6	8	9	2
6	9	1	8	7	2	4	5	3
5	8	2	3	9	4	7	1	6

101

7	1	8	5	9	4	3	2	6
3	6	2	8	1	7	4	5	9
9	5	4	2	6	3	8	7	1
6	8	1	4	5	9	7	3	2
4	2	9	7	3	1	6	8	5
5	7	3	6	2	8	9	1	4
2	3	6	9	8	5	1	4	7
1	4	5	3	7	6	2	9	8
8	9	7	1	4	2	5	6	3

102

6	7	5	9	3	4	2	1	8
9	1	8	6	5	2	3	7	4
2	3	4	7	8	1	9	6	5
5	6	9	2	1	3	4	8	7
4	2	7	5	6	8	1	3	9
3	8	1	4	9	7	5	2	6
1	5	2	8	4	6	7	9	3
8	4	3	1	7	9	6	5	2
7	9	6	3	2	5	8	4	1

103

2	1	4	3	6	5	9	8	7
7	6	5	2	9	8	3	4	1
3	8	9	7	1	4	6	2	5
4	3	1	6	5	2	8	7	9
5	9	6	4	8	7	1	3	2
8	7	2	9	3	1	4	5	6
9	2	7	8	4	6	5	1	3
6	5	8	1	7	3	2	9	4
1	4	3	5	2	9	7	6	8

104

9	7	3	1	5	4	2	8	6
8	1	5	2	3	6	7	4	9
6	2	4	7	8	9	1	5	3
7	3	8	6	9	1	4	2	5
4	9	1	8	2	5	6	3	7
5	6	2	4	7	3	8	9	1
3	8	6	5	4	7	9	1	2
1	4	9	3	6	2	5	7	8
2	5	7	9	1	8	3	6	4

105

5	8	9	3	4	1	2	6	7
2	4	6	9	8	7	1	5	3
3	7	1	5	2	6	4	8	9
7	5	3	4	6	8	9	1	2
9	1	8	2	7	3	6	4	5
4	6	2	1	5	9	3	7	8
6	9	4	7	3	5	8	2	1
8	3	7	6	1	2	5	9	4
1	2	5	8	9	4	7	3	6

106

3	2	1	6	5	8	7	9	4
6	5	4	3	7	9	2	1	8
9	8	7	2	1	4	3	6	5
2	6	5	8	4	1	9	3	7
4	1	8	7	9	3	6	5	2
7	9	3	5	2	6	4	8	1
8	7	9	4	6	5	1	2	3
5	4	6	1	3	2	8	7	9
1	3	2	9	8	7	5	4	6

107

5	7	6	4	8	2	3	9	1
3	4	8	9	7	1	2	6	5
1	9	2	5	6	3	8	4	7
7	1	9	2	3	6	4	5	8
6	3	5	1	4	8	7	2	9
8	2	4	7	9	5	6	1	3
2	8	1	3	5	4	9	7	6
9	5	3	6	2	7	1	8	4
4	6	7	8	1	9	5	3	2

108

6	8	7	1	9	3	4	2	5
5	4	2	6	8	7	1	9	3
9	3	1	4	5	2	8	6	7
7	9	3	2	4	8	5	1	6
8	1	5	9	7	6	2	3	4
4	2	6	3	1	5	7	8	9
2	6	8	5	3	4	9	7	1
3	5	9	7	2	1	6	4	8
1	7	4	8	6	9	3	5	2

109

1	6	7	3	8	5	2	4	9
9	3	8	7	4	2	6	5	1
4	2	5	1	6	9	7	3	8
3	7	9	4	5	6	8	1	2
6	4	2	9	1	8	5	7	3
8	5	1	2	7	3	4	9	6
5	1	3	6	2	4	9	8	7
7	8	6	5	9	1	3	2	4
2	9	4	8	3	7	1	6	5

110

3	4	5	2	8	9	7	6	1
1	7	8	3	6	4	9	2	5
9	6	2	1	5	7	8	4	3
7	9	3	6	1	5	4	8	2
5	2	6	9	4	8	1	3	7
4	8	1	7	2	3	5	9	6
6	5	7	4	9	2	3	1	8
2	3	9	8	7	1	6	5	4
8	1	4	5	3	6	2	7	9

111

2	4	5	6	3	9	7	1	8
9	6	8	4	7	1	3	2	5
7	1	3	8	2	5	9	6	4
5	3	1	9	4	6	2	8	7
4	7	6	3	8	2	1	5	9
8	2	9	5	1	7	4	3	6
1	5	4	2	9	8	6	7	3
3	8	7	1	6	4	5	9	2
6	9	2	7	5	3	8	4	1

112

6	7	1	3	5	4	8	9	2
4	9	2	8	1	6	3	7	5
8	3	5	9	7	2	1	6	4
3	8	6	7	2	9	5	4	1
5	2	9	4	6	1	7	3	8
7	1	4	5	3	8	6	2	9
1	4	7	2	8	3	9	5	6
9	6	3	1	4	5	2	8	7
2	5	8	6	9	7	4	1	3

2	9	7	1	5	4	3	8	6
6	8	4	3	7	9	5	1	2
1	5	3	6	8	2	9	7	4
9	3	6	4	2	8	1	5	7
5	7	8	9	1	6	4	2	3
4	2	1	7	3	5	6	9	8
7	6	9	8	4	1	2	3	5
3	1	2	5	6	7	8	4	9
8	4	5	2	9	3	7	6	1

9	7	4	1	6	3	2	5	8
2	8	6	5	9	4	7	1	3
1	3	5	8	7	2	4	6	9
6	4	1	7	3	8	5	9	2
8	9	7	6	2	5	3	4	1
5	2	3	4	1	9	8	7	6
3	5	2	9	4	1	6	8	7
7	1	8	3	5	6	9	2	4
4	6	9	2	8	7	1	3	5

6	7	3	2	9	5	8	4	1
9	5	1	8	7	4	6	3	2
4	2	8	6	1	3	5	9	7
3	4	7	1	2	6	9	5	8
5	9	6	4	8	7	1	2	3
8	1	2	3	5	9	7	6	4
2	8	5	9	3	1	4	7	6
7	3	4	5	6	8	2	1	9
1	6	9	7	4	2	3	8	5

8	2	7	3	6	4	9	5	1
4	3	6	5	1	9	2	7	8
9	1	5	7	2	8	4	6	3
3	9	8	2	5	1	6	4	7
7	5	2	6	4	3	8	1	9
1	6	4	9	8	7	3	2	5
6	4	3	8	7	5	1	9	2
2	7	9	1	3	6	5	8	4
5	8	1	4	9	2	7	3	6

4	6	2	7	1	5	8	9	3
1	5	3	8	2	9	7	4	6
8	9	7	3	6	4	2	1	5
6	1	4	2	5	3	9	8	7
7	2	8	6	9	1	5	3	4
5	3	9	4	7	8	6	2	1
9	8	5	1	4	6	3	7	2
3	7	1	5	8	2	4	6	9
2	4	6	9	3	7	1	5	8

1	2	3	6	5	7	4	8	9
6	5	8	3	4	9	1	2	7
4	7	9	2	8	1	5	3	6
5	1	4	9	3	2	7	6	8
8	6	2	7	1	5	3	9	4
3	9	7	8	6	4	2	1	5
2	4	5	1	9	6	8	7	3
9	3	1	5	7	8	6	4	2
7	8	6	4	2	3	9	5	1

8	1	2	5	9	3	4	7	6
7	3	6	8	4	1	9	2	5
4	5	9	2	6	7	8	3	1
2	9	1	6	3	5	7	4	8
6	7	5	9	8	4	2	1	3
3	4	8	1	7	2	6	5	9
9	2	4	3	5	6	1	8	7
5	8	7	4	1	9	3	6	2
1	6	3	7	2	8	5	9	4

8	1	6	7	2	3	5	4	9
5	4	3	1	8	9	6	2	7
9	7	2	5	6	4	8	3	1
2	5	4	8	1	7	9	6	3
7	6	1	9	3	2	4	8	5
3	8	9	6	4	5	7	1	2
6	9	8	2	5	1	3	7	4
4	2	5	3	7	6	1	9	8
1	3	7	4	9	8	2	5	6

Puzzle 121

7	8	1	9	6	4	5	2	3
4	9	5	3	7	2	1	8	6
6	2	3	5	1	8	7	9	4
8	3	2	1	4	9	6	7	5
9	7	6	8	3	5	2	4	1
1	5	4	6	2	7	8	3	9
2	6	8	4	9	1	3	5	7
5	1	9	7	8	3	4	6	2
3	4	7	2	5	6	9	1	8

Puzzle 122

1	5	2	3	7	9	4	8	6
3	8	6	5	1	4	7	9	2
4	7	9	8	2	6	1	5	3
2	4	3	9	6	1	8	7	5
6	1	7	4	8	5	2	3	9
8	9	5	2	3	7	6	4	1
5	2	8	6	4	3	9	1	7
9	6	1	7	5	8	3	2	4
7	3	4	1	9	2	5	6	8

Puzzle 123

4	1	8	5	3	7	6	9	2
3	2	7	6	8	9	5	1	4
5	6	9	1	2	4	7	8	3
6	4	2	3	9	5	8	7	1
7	8	3	2	6	1	9	4	5
9	5	1	4	7	8	3	2	6
2	7	5	8	4	6	1	3	9
8	3	6	9	1	2	4	5	7
1	9	4	7	5	3	2	6	8

Puzzle 124

2	9	5	3	7	8	4	1	6
7	4	6	1	2	9	3	8	5
1	8	3	5	4	6	9	7	2
4	7	1	6	8	2	5	9	3
5	2	8	7	9	3	1	6	4
6	3	9	4	5	1	8	2	7
8	6	7	9	3	5	2	4	1
9	5	4	2	1	7	6	3	8
3	1	2	8	6	4	7	5	9

Puzzle 125

7	3	4	5	9	1	6	8	2
8	5	2	7	4	6	1	9	3
9	6	1	3	2	8	7	4	5
3	9	5	6	7	4	8	2	1
4	8	6	9	1	2	5	3	7
1	2	7	8	5	3	9	6	4
6	7	3	4	8	5	2	1	9
5	1	8	2	3	9	4	7	6
2	4	9	1	6	7	3	5	8

Puzzle 126

1	4	2	3	9	6	5	8	7
3	5	6	8	7	1	4	9	2
9	8	7	2	5	4	3	6	1
6	9	4	1	3	7	8	2	5
8	2	5	4	6	9	1	7	3
7	3	1	5	2	8	6	4	9
5	6	9	7	4	3	2	1	8
4	1	3	9	8	2	7	5	6
2	7	8	6	1	5	9	3	4

Puzzle 127

8	7	5	4	3	1	6	9	2
3	9	6	7	2	8	5	1	4
2	1	4	6	5	9	3	8	7
1	8	3	9	7	5	4	2	6
5	2	7	8	4	6	1	3	9
4	6	9	2	1	3	8	7	5
7	5	1	3	6	2	9	4	8
6	4	8	1	9	7	2	5	3
9	3	2	5	8	4	7	6	1

Puzzle 128

8	1	6	2	5	9	4	7	3
5	3	2	6	4	7	1	9	8
7	9	4	1	8	3	2	5	6
1	8	9	7	3	5	6	2	4
3	2	7	4	6	8	9	1	5
6	4	5	9	1	2	8	3	7
2	5	8	3	9	6	7	4	1
9	6	1	5	7	4	3	8	2
4	7	3	8	2	1	5	6	9

129

9	7	3	6	8	5	4	1	2
2	4	8	1	7	3	5	6	9
5	1	6	2	9	4	7	8	3
6	3	2	8	1	7	9	5	4
1	9	5	4	6	2	3	7	8
7	8	4	5	3	9	6	2	1
8	6	7	9	4	1	2	3	5
4	5	1	3	2	6	8	9	7
3	2	9	7	5	8	1	4	6

130

6	4	8	5	2	3	9	7	1
3	9	1	6	7	8	5	2	4
7	2	5	9	1	4	6	8	3
1	8	3	4	6	2	7	5	9
2	5	6	7	9	1	3	4	8
4	7	9	3	8	5	1	6	2
5	3	7	8	4	9	2	1	6
9	1	4	2	5	6	8	3	7
8	6	2	1	3	7	4	9	5

131

8	4	9	5	2	1	3	6	7
1	2	7	9	3	6	5	8	4
5	3	6	4	7	8	1	9	2
7	9	4	3	8	5	6	2	1
6	1	2	7	9	4	8	3	5
3	8	5	6	1	2	4	7	9
2	7	1	8	5	3	9	4	6
9	6	8	1	4	7	2	5	3
4	5	3	2	6	9	7	1	8

132

4	9	6	5	1	3	8	2	7
7	2	3	4	8	9	1	5	6
8	5	1	2	6	7	4	9	3
5	7	8	3	9	2	6	4	1
1	4	2	8	7	6	5	3	9
3	6	9	1	5	4	7	8	2
9	1	5	7	3	8	2	6	4
2	3	7	6	4	5	9	1	8
6	8	4	9	2	1	3	7	5

133

2	6	4	7	5	9	3	1	8
8	1	9	4	2	3	7	6	5
7	3	5	1	6	8	2	4	9
1	8	6	9	4	2	5	7	3
4	7	2	6	3	5	9	8	1
9	5	3	8	1	7	6	2	4
5	9	7	2	8	1	4	3	6
6	2	1	3	9	4	8	5	7
3	4	8	5	7	6	1	9	2

134

6	4	5	1	7	2	3	8	9
7	8	3	9	6	4	5	1	2
1	2	9	8	5	3	6	4	7
9	7	2	6	3	8	1	5	4
8	3	4	7	1	5	2	9	6
5	1	6	2	4	9	8	7	3
3	6	1	5	9	7	4	2	8
4	9	8	3	2	1	7	6	5
2	5	7	4	8	6	9	3	1

135

4	5	8	3	2	7	9	1	6
7	6	2	5	1	9	4	3	8
1	3	9	8	6	4	7	2	5
6	1	5	4	9	3	8	7	2
8	4	7	6	5	2	3	9	1
2	9	3	1	7	8	5	6	4
9	2	6	7	8	5	1	4	3
5	7	4	2	3	1	6	8	9
3	8	1	9	4	6	2	5	7

136

4	8	1	2	6	9	7	3	5
6	9	5	8	7	3	1	2	4
3	7	2	5	4	1	6	8	9
5	3	9	4	1	7	2	6	8
8	1	7	9	2	6	4	5	3
2	4	6	3	8	5	9	7	1
9	6	4	7	3	8	5	1	2
1	2	3	6	5	4	8	9	7
7	5	8	1	9	2	3	4	6

137

1	4	7	8	2	6	9	3	5
2	6	3	1	9	5	4	8	7
8	9	5	4	3	7	2	1	6
6	2	8	3	4	1	7	5	9
5	1	9	7	6	2	8	4	3
7	3	4	9	5	8	6	2	1
4	8	1	5	7	9	3	6	2
3	7	2	6	1	4	5	9	8
9	5	6	2	8	3	1	7	4

138

9	4	5	8	1	7	2	6	3
6	1	2	9	3	5	4	7	8
3	8	7	2	6	4	9	1	5
4	2	9	7	5	8	1	3	6
5	3	8	1	2	6	7	4	9
7	6	1	4	9	3	5	8	2
1	9	4	6	8	2	3	5	7
2	5	6	3	7	1	8	9	4
8	7	3	5	4	9	6	2	1

139

4	8	9	7	6	5	3	1	2
2	1	3	8	9	4	5	6	7
6	5	7	2	1	3	4	8	9
7	3	4	1	8	9	2	5	6
9	6	1	5	4	2	8	7	3
8	2	5	3	7	6	1	9	4
3	4	6	9	5	1	7	2	8
1	9	8	4	2	7	6	3	5
5	7	2	6	3	8	9	4	1

140

9	1	8	5	4	3	6	7	2
4	6	7	8	9	2	3	5	1
5	2	3	1	7	6	4	9	8
7	8	2	4	6	9	1	3	5
6	5	4	2	3	1	9	8	7
1	3	9	7	8	5	2	4	6
8	9	6	3	2	7	5	1	4
3	7	1	6	5	4	8	2	9
2	4	5	9	1	8	7	6	3

141

2	1	6	9	7	5	3	8	4
4	3	8	2	1	6	5	7	9
5	7	9	3	8	4	6	2	1
1	8	7	5	4	9	2	6	3
9	5	3	7	6	2	1	4	8
6	4	2	1	3	8	9	5	7
3	9	4	6	2	7	8	1	5
8	2	1	4	5	3	7	9	6
7	6	5	8	9	1	4	3	2

142

8	3	4	1	9	7	2	6	5
7	9	1	6	2	5	3	4	8
6	2	5	4	3	8	7	9	1
3	4	9	7	6	1	8	5	2
2	1	6	5	8	9	4	7	3
5	8	7	3	4	2	9	1	6
1	5	3	2	7	4	6	8	9
4	6	8	9	1	3	5	2	7
9	7	2	8	5	6	1	3	4

143

5	3	2	4	9	7	1	8	6
4	9	7	8	1	6	5	3	2
8	1	6	3	5	2	7	4	9
2	8	1	5	3	4	6	9	7
3	5	9	6	7	1	8	2	4
7	6	4	9	2	8	3	1	5
9	4	8	1	6	5	2	7	3
6	2	3	7	8	9	4	5	1
1	7	5	2	4	3	9	6	8

144

1	7	5	2	9	3	8	6	4
6	9	3	4	8	7	5	2	1
4	8	2	6	5	1	9	3	7
2	5	8	7	3	9	1	4	6
9	3	6	1	2	4	7	5	8
7	1	4	5	6	8	3	9	2
3	6	1	8	4	5	2	7	9
8	4	9	3	7	2	6	1	5
5	2	7	9	1	6	4	8	3

145

9	5	6	1	4	2	8	3	7
1	2	7	9	8	3	4	6	5
3	8	4	5	7	6	9	2	1
6	3	5	8	1	9	7	4	2
7	1	2	3	6	4	5	9	8
4	9	8	7	2	5	6	1	3
2	4	1	6	5	8	3	7	9
5	6	9	2	3	7	1	8	4
8	7	3	4	9	1	2	5	6

146

6	3	2	8	4	1	5	9	7
1	9	7	3	2	5	4	8	6
5	4	8	6	9	7	3	1	2
2	5	4	1	6	8	7	3	9
3	6	9	2	7	4	1	5	8
8	7	1	9	5	3	6	2	4
9	8	3	7	1	6	2	4	5
4	2	6	5	3	9	8	7	1
7	1	5	4	8	2	9	6	3

147

3	7	4	2	9	5	8	6	1
1	2	8	6	3	7	9	4	5
5	9	6	4	1	8	7	3	2
2	8	9	7	5	4	6	1	3
6	5	7	1	2	3	4	8	9
4	1	3	9	8	6	2	5	7
7	6	1	3	4	9	5	2	8
8	4	2	5	7	1	3	9	6
9	3	5	8	6	2	1	7	4

148

2	5	3	7	9	8	1	4	6
6	9	4	1	3	2	8	7	5
7	8	1	4	6	5	2	3	9
5	1	9	3	8	7	4	6	2
8	4	7	6	2	1	5	9	3
3	2	6	5	4	9	7	1	8
9	7	8	2	1	3	6	5	4
4	3	5	8	7	6	9	2	1
1	6	2	9	5	4	3	8	7

149

9	2	7	5	4	6	1	8	3
4	6	5	1	8	3	9	2	7
3	1	8	2	9	7	5	4	6
1	9	6	4	2	5	7	3	8
8	5	2	3	7	1	6	9	4
7	4	3	8	6	9	2	5	1
5	7	1	9	3	8	4	6	2
6	8	4	7	5	2	3	1	9
2	3	9	6	1	4	8	7	5

150

6	4	5	7	3	9	1	8	2
1	2	3	8	5	6	4	7	9
7	8	9	4	1	2	6	5	3
5	6	8	1	7	3	9	2	4
9	7	1	2	8	4	5	3	6
4	3	2	9	6	5	7	1	8
3	5	7	6	4	8	2	9	1
8	9	6	5	2	1	3	4	7
2	1	4	3	9	7	8	6	5

151

9	6	8	4	3	2	1	5	7
5	2	7	6	1	8	4	9	3
4	3	1	7	5	9	2	6	8
3	9	4	2	8	6	7	1	5
6	7	2	5	4	1	3	8	9
8	1	5	3	9	7	6	4	2
1	5	6	9	2	3	8	7	4
2	8	9	1	7	4	5	3	6
7	4	3	8	6	5	9	2	1

152

6	5	3	7	9	2	4	1	8
2	1	7	8	5	4	9	6	3
8	9	4	6	1	3	2	5	7
1	3	5	4	7	9	6	8	2
7	4	6	1	2	8	5	3	9
9	2	8	3	6	5	7	4	1
3	7	9	5	4	1	8	2	6
4	6	1	2	8	7	3	9	5
5	8	2	9	3	6	1	7	4

153

7	8	2	9	5	4	6	1	3
9	1	5	8	6	3	4	7	2
3	6	4	2	7	1	5	8	9
4	2	6	7	1	8	3	9	5
8	7	3	4	9	5	2	6	1
5	9	1	6	3	2	8	4	7
2	3	7	1	4	6	9	5	8
6	5	9	3	8	7	1	2	4
1	4	8	5	2	9	7	3	6

154

2	7	5	6	4	1	9	3	8
6	1	3	5	8	9	4	7	2
8	9	4	7	3	2	1	6	5
3	5	8	2	6	4	7	9	1
1	6	9	8	5	7	3	2	4
4	2	7	1	9	3	5	8	6
5	8	1	9	7	6	2	4	3
9	3	6	4	2	5	8	1	7
7	4	2	3	1	8	6	5	9

155

5	4	3	2	1	6	8	7	9
2	1	8	9	3	7	4	6	5
7	9	6	8	5	4	1	3	2
3	6	7	1	8	2	5	9	4
1	8	4	7	9	5	3	2	6
9	5	2	6	4	3	7	8	1
4	3	9	5	2	8	6	1	7
8	7	1	4	6	9	2	5	3
6	2	5	3	7	1	9	4	8

156

7	8	9	6	5	4	3	2	1
1	4	6	9	3	2	5	7	8
2	5	3	8	7	1	6	4	9
8	6	1	7	2	3	9	5	4
5	7	2	4	1	9	8	6	3
3	9	4	5	6	8	2	1	7
4	3	7	2	8	6	1	9	5
9	2	8	1	4	5	7	3	6
6	1	5	3	9	7	4	8	2

157

2	1	8	7	6	9	4	3	5
9	3	6	8	4	5	2	1	7
5	4	7	3	2	1	8	9	6
4	8	5	6	7	3	1	2	9
7	6	1	2	9	4	5	8	3
3	9	2	5	1	8	7	6	4
8	5	9	1	3	7	6	4	2
6	7	4	9	8	2	3	5	1
1	2	3	4	5	6	9	7	8

158

3	7	9	4	5	6	2	8	1
5	4	6	8	2	1	9	3	7
2	8	1	9	7	3	4	5	6
9	3	8	1	6	5	7	2	4
7	6	5	2	3	4	1	9	8
1	2	4	7	8	9	5	6	3
6	5	2	3	4	7	8	1	9
4	1	3	5	9	8	6	7	2
8	9	7	6	1	2	3	4	5

159

8	9	5	1	7	2	3	6	4
1	2	4	3	6	9	7	5	8
3	7	6	4	8	5	1	2	9
2	8	1	7	3	4	6	9	5
5	6	3	9	1	8	4	7	2
9	4	7	2	5	6	8	3	1
4	3	8	5	2	7	9	1	6
6	1	2	8	9	3	5	4	7
7	5	9	6	4	1	2	8	3

160

7	8	3	2	4	5	9	1	6
2	5	9	7	1	6	4	3	8
6	1	4	9	3	8	7	2	5
3	2	1	4	5	7	6	8	9
4	9	6	1	8	2	3	5	7
5	7	8	3	6	9	2	4	1
9	6	5	8	2	4	1	7	3
1	4	7	5	9	3	8	6	2
8	3	2	6	7	1	5	9	4

161

8	2	1	7	4	9	3	5	6
5	7	9	2	6	3	8	1	4
3	6	4	8	1	5	9	2	7
1	5	7	3	2	8	6	4	9
2	8	6	1	9	4	5	7	3
9	4	3	6	5	7	1	8	2
4	9	8	5	7	6	2	3	1
6	3	2	4	8	1	7	9	5
7	1	5	9	3	2	4	6	8

162

4	9	5	2	8	1	6	7	3
3	1	6	9	5	7	2	4	8
2	8	7	3	4	6	1	5	9
9	3	2	7	6	4	5	8	1
6	5	1	8	2	9	4	3	7
7	4	8	5	1	3	9	6	2
8	6	3	4	9	2	7	1	5
5	2	4	1	7	8	3	9	6
1	7	9	6	3	5	8	2	4

163

8	5	6	7	9	3	2	1	4
2	9	7	6	4	1	5	8	3
3	4	1	2	8	5	7	6	9
9	3	2	4	7	8	6	5	1
7	8	5	1	3	6	4	9	2
1	6	4	9	5	2	3	7	8
4	7	3	8	6	9	1	2	5
5	2	9	3	1	7	8	4	6
6	1	8	5	2	4	9	3	7

164

5	7	1	4	2	8	9	6	3
2	9	4	6	3	1	7	5	8
3	8	6	5	7	9	2	1	4
8	2	7	3	4	5	6	9	1
4	6	3	1	9	7	8	2	5
9	1	5	2	8	6	3	4	7
6	3	8	9	5	4	1	7	2
1	4	2	7	6	3	5	8	9
7	5	9	8	1	2	4	3	6

165

2	4	6	7	3	5	8	9	1
5	8	9	1	2	4	7	3	6
1	3	7	9	8	6	4	2	5
4	6	5	8	1	3	2	7	9
9	1	8	2	5	7	6	4	3
3	7	2	6	4	9	5	1	8
7	9	3	4	6	8	1	5	2
8	5	1	3	7	2	9	6	4
6	2	4	5	9	1	3	8	7

166

7	6	3	5	2	4	1	8	9
4	5	2	1	8	9	6	7	3
8	9	1	6	7	3	4	2	5
9	3	6	2	5	1	8	4	7
1	2	7	3	4	8	9	5	6
5	4	8	9	6	7	3	1	2
2	7	9	4	1	6	5	3	8
6	8	4	7	3	5	2	9	1
3	1	5	8	9	2	7	6	4

167

2	1	3	7	6	5	9	4	8
6	8	5	9	2	4	7	1	3
7	4	9	3	1	8	6	2	5
8	3	2	4	7	1	5	6	9
9	5	1	2	3	6	4	8	7
4	7	6	8	5	9	2	3	1
3	6	8	5	9	2	1	7	4
1	9	7	6	4	3	8	5	2
5	2	4	1	8	7	3	9	6

168

5	3	2	6	8	4	9	7	1
6	4	7	2	9	1	3	8	5
9	1	8	7	3	5	2	4	6
1	2	6	5	7	3	4	9	8
8	9	4	1	6	2	7	5	3
3	7	5	8	4	9	6	1	2
4	5	9	3	1	6	8	2	7
7	6	1	9	2	8	5	3	4
2	8	3	4	5	7	1	6	9

169

9	6	1	7	5	3	8	2	4
8	7	3	2	4	9	6	1	5
2	5	4	1	8	6	7	3	9
1	4	7	9	6	2	5	8	3
3	9	6	5	7	8	1	4	2
5	8	2	4	3	1	9	7	6
7	2	8	3	9	5	4	6	1
6	1	9	8	2	4	3	5	7
4	3	5	6	1	7	2	9	8

170

1	6	9	3	2	7	8	5	4
3	4	8	1	6	5	9	7	2
5	7	2	9	8	4	3	6	1
2	5	1	6	3	8	7	4	9
7	9	3	2	4	1	6	8	5
4	8	6	5	7	9	2	1	3
9	3	4	7	5	6	1	2	8
8	1	7	4	9	2	5	3	6
6	2	5	8	1	3	4	9	7

171

9	3	7	2	8	1	5	4	6
1	5	6	7	4	9	2	8	3
4	2	8	6	5	3	9	1	7
7	8	4	9	1	2	3	6	5
2	9	5	4	3	6	1	7	8
6	1	3	5	7	8	4	2	9
5	4	1	8	9	7	6	3	2
3	7	2	1	6	5	8	9	4
8	6	9	3	2	4	7	5	1

172

5	2	8	3	4	7	6	1	9
1	3	7	5	9	6	8	2	4
9	4	6	2	8	1	3	7	5
2	9	1	8	3	5	4	6	7
3	7	5	4	6	2	1	9	8
8	6	4	1	7	9	5	3	2
6	5	9	7	1	4	2	8	3
7	8	2	6	5	3	9	4	1
4	1	3	9	2	8	7	5	6

173

1	2	7	9	6	5	8	4	3
5	8	6	2	4	3	7	9	1
4	9	3	8	7	1	2	6	5
8	3	5	1	2	4	9	7	6
6	1	4	5	9	7	3	2	8
9	7	2	6	3	8	5	1	4
2	4	9	3	8	6	1	5	7
7	5	8	4	1	9	6	3	2
3	6	1	7	5	2	4	8	9

174

8	1	2	4	5	7	3	9	6
4	6	9	3	2	8	1	5	7
7	3	5	6	9	1	4	2	8
1	2	8	5	3	9	6	7	4
9	4	3	7	6	2	5	8	1
5	7	6	8	1	4	9	3	2
2	9	7	1	4	3	8	6	5
6	8	4	9	7	5	2	1	3
3	5	1	2	8	6	7	4	9

175

2	4	1	5	3	6	8	9	7
8	7	6	1	9	2	3	4	5
3	5	9	8	7	4	2	6	1
6	1	7	9	8	5	4	3	2
5	9	8	2	4	3	7	1	6
4	2	3	6	1	7	5	8	9
1	6	5	4	2	8	9	7	3
7	8	2	3	6	9	1	5	4
9	3	4	7	5	1	6	2	8

176

1	3	4	5	2	6	8	9	7
6	5	9	4	7	8	1	3	2
2	8	7	3	1	9	6	5	4
4	9	8	1	6	5	2	7	3
5	6	3	2	8	7	4	1	9
7	2	1	9	4	3	5	6	8
3	7	6	8	5	2	9	4	1
9	1	2	6	3	4	7	8	5
8	4	5	7	9	1	3	2	6

177

1	7	9	2	4	6	8	5	3
4	2	8	9	3	5	7	6	1
5	3	6	8	7	1	4	9	2
7	1	4	6	2	3	5	8	9
3	9	5	4	8	7	1	2	6
8	6	2	1	5	9	3	4	7
2	8	7	3	9	4	6	1	5
9	5	1	7	6	8	2	3	4
6	4	3	5	1	2	9	7	8

178

7	3	8	4	5	9	2	6	1
6	2	5	3	8	1	4	9	7
1	9	4	7	6	2	3	5	8
4	7	9	1	3	8	6	2	5
3	5	6	9	2	7	8	1	4
2	8	1	5	4	6	7	3	9
9	6	2	8	7	5	1	4	3
5	4	7	6	1	3	9	8	2
8	1	3	2	9	4	5	7	6

179

1	3	6	8	2	9	5	7	4
7	9	4	6	5	3	1	8	2
5	8	2	7	4	1	9	3	6
9	5	3	2	1	6	8	4	7
8	2	7	5	9	4	3	6	1
4	6	1	3	7	8	2	5	9
6	7	8	1	3	2	4	9	5
3	1	9	4	6	5	7	2	8
2	4	5	9	8	7	6	1	3

180

6	1	8	9	3	4	2	5	7
2	4	7	6	5	1	3	9	8
5	3	9	8	7	2	4	1	6
9	6	4	2	1	8	7	3	5
1	8	3	7	4	5	6	2	9
7	5	2	3	9	6	1	8	4
8	9	6	4	2	3	5	7	1
3	7	1	5	6	9	8	4	2
4	2	5	1	8	7	9	6	3

181

8	4	3	9	1	2	5	6	7
6	2	9	3	5	7	1	4	8
5	7	1	4	8	6	3	9	2
3	5	6	8	2	1	9	7	4
9	8	4	5	7	3	6	2	1
7	1	2	6	4	9	8	5	3
4	9	7	1	6	8	2	3	5
2	6	8	7	3	5	4	1	9
1	3	5	2	9	4	7	8	6

182

5	4	7	1	2	9	6	8	3
2	3	1	6	8	7	4	9	5
6	8	9	5	3	4	2	1	7
9	7	6	2	1	5	3	4	8
3	2	4	8	7	6	1	5	9
8	1	5	4	9	3	7	6	2
1	6	3	7	5	8	9	2	4
7	5	2	9	4	1	8	3	6
4	9	8	3	6	2	5	7	1

183

8	1	7	3	6	9	2	4	5
5	6	3	2	1	4	9	8	7
9	2	4	5	7	8	6	3	1
4	5	1	6	2	3	8	7	9
6	8	9	1	4	7	5	2	3
7	3	2	9	8	5	1	6	4
1	4	6	7	9	2	3	5	8
3	9	8	4	5	6	7	1	2
2	7	5	8	3	1	4	9	6

184

4	6	5	1	2	7	8	9	3
7	1	3	4	9	8	6	5	2
2	9	8	5	6	3	4	1	7
3	5	4	9	1	2	7	6	8
1	8	7	6	3	5	9	2	4
6	2	9	7	8	4	5	3	1
5	3	6	8	7	1	2	4	9
8	4	2	3	5	9	1	7	6
9	7	1	2	4	6	3	8	5

185

6	7	5	4	8	2	9	3	1
4	1	8	3	6	9	5	7	2
2	3	9	7	5	1	6	4	8
1	8	3	5	2	7	4	9	6
7	4	6	1	9	8	2	5	3
9	5	2	6	4	3	1	8	7
5	2	1	8	3	4	7	6	9
8	9	4	2	7	6	3	1	5
3	6	7	9	1	5	8	2	4

186

9	1	5	3	6	8	4	2	7
6	3	8	2	4	7	5	1	9
7	4	2	9	1	5	6	8	3
5	2	7	1	3	9	8	4	6
1	9	4	7	8	6	2	3	5
8	6	3	4	5	2	9	7	1
3	8	1	5	9	4	7	6	2
4	7	9	6	2	1	3	5	8
2	5	6	8	7	3	1	9	4

187

4	6	1	3	8	7	9	2	5
2	9	7	6	1	5	8	3	4
3	5	8	4	2	9	6	1	7
1	4	5	7	6	8	2	9	3
8	2	9	5	4	3	1	7	6
7	3	6	1	9	2	5	4	8
6	1	3	2	5	4	7	8	9
5	8	4	9	7	1	3	6	2
9	7	2	8	3	6	4	5	1

188

2	9	7	5	1	8	6	3	4
4	3	8	6	7	9	2	1	5
6	1	5	4	2	3	9	8	7
8	5	4	1	3	2	7	9	6
3	6	1	9	4	7	5	2	8
7	2	9	8	5	6	3	4	1
1	4	3	2	6	5	8	7	9
9	7	6	3	8	4	1	5	2
5	8	2	7	9	1	4	6	3

189

7	5	4	9	1	8	2	6	3
9	1	6	4	2	3	5	7	8
8	2	3	7	6	5	4	9	1
2	9	8	6	3	7	1	5	4
3	6	7	5	4	1	9	8	2
1	4	5	8	9	2	6	3	7
4	7	1	3	5	6	8	2	9
5	3	9	2	8	4	7	1	6
6	8	2	1	7	9	3	4	5

190

7	9	2	3	8	6	4	1	5
4	8	5	9	2	1	6	7	3
3	6	1	7	4	5	2	8	9
2	4	6	5	7	8	3	9	1
1	7	9	4	3	2	5	6	8
5	3	8	6	1	9	7	4	2
8	1	7	2	6	3	9	5	4
9	2	4	1	5	7	8	3	6
6	5	3	8	9	4	1	2	7

191

8	2	7	4	5	1	6	9	3
6	5	1	8	3	9	7	2	4
9	3	4	2	6	7	1	8	5
7	9	6	1	8	3	5	4	2
3	1	5	6	2	4	8	7	9
4	8	2	7	9	5	3	6	1
1	7	8	5	4	2	9	3	6
5	4	9	3	7	6	2	1	8
2	6	3	9	1	8	4	5	7

192

6	5	3	1	7	4	8	9	2
2	8	9	3	6	5	4	1	7
7	1	4	8	2	9	6	5	3
3	9	2	4	1	8	7	6	5
8	6	7	9	5	2	3	4	1
1	4	5	7	3	6	2	8	9
9	2	6	5	4	7	1	3	8
5	7	1	6	8	3	9	2	4
4	3	8	2	9	1	5	7	6

193

5	9	8	4	1	7	6	2	3
4	3	1	8	6	2	7	9	5
6	7	2	3	9	5	4	1	8
3	8	4	9	7	6	2	5	1
2	1	6	5	3	8	9	7	4
7	5	9	1	2	4	8	3	6
8	6	7	2	5	3	1	4	9
1	2	3	6	4	9	5	8	7
9	4	5	7	8	1	3	6	2

194

4	2	1	8	3	9	5	7	6
9	7	8	2	6	5	1	4	3
5	3	6	1	4	7	2	8	9
3	8	2	6	7	4	9	1	5
7	1	5	9	2	3	4	6	8
6	9	4	5	1	8	7	3	2
1	6	3	4	9	2	8	5	7
2	5	7	3	8	1	6	9	4
8	4	9	7	5	6	3	2	1

195

7	9	3	1	2	6	8	4	5
8	4	5	7	9	3	6	2	1
6	2	1	5	4	8	3	9	7
9	6	8	4	7	2	5	1	3
3	7	2	8	5	1	4	6	9
1	5	4	3	6	9	7	8	2
5	1	9	6	8	7	2	3	4
2	8	7	9	3	4	1	5	6
4	3	6	2	1	5	9	7	8

196

8	6	2	1	5	4	9	3	7
9	4	3	7	2	8	1	6	5
5	1	7	3	9	6	4	8	2
2	7	4	9	8	5	3	1	6
3	5	9	2	6	1	7	4	8
1	8	6	4	7	3	2	5	9
7	3	8	6	4	2	5	9	1
4	9	5	8	1	7	6	2	3
6	2	1	5	3	9	8	7	4

197

9	7	1	5	4	6	8	3	2
8	4	6	7	2	3	5	1	9
2	5	3	1	8	9	4	7	6
6	8	7	9	3	5	2	4	1
5	2	9	6	1	4	7	8	3
3	1	4	2	7	8	6	9	5
1	6	5	8	9	7	3	2	4
4	9	8	3	6	2	1	5	7
7	3	2	4	5	1	9	6	8

198

6	1	8	3	5	9	4	7	2
4	7	3	8	1	2	5	9	6
2	9	5	4	6	7	3	8	1
1	2	4	5	9	3	7	6	8
5	8	6	1	7	4	9	2	3
7	3	9	2	8	6	1	5	4
8	4	2	7	3	5	6	1	9
3	6	7	9	2	1	8	4	5
9	5	1	6	4	8	2	3	7

199

8	7	2	5	3	6	9	1	4
1	9	3	7	8	4	6	5	2
6	5	4	9	1	2	3	8	7
3	2	9	6	4	1	8	7	5
4	1	8	3	7	5	2	9	6
7	6	5	2	9	8	4	3	1
2	3	6	8	5	7	1	4	9
5	8	1	4	6	9	7	2	3
9	4	7	1	2	3	5	6	8

200

7	6	3	2	5	8	4	9	1
2	4	1	7	6	9	5	8	3
9	8	5	4	1	3	7	6	2
4	9	7	1	8	6	3	2	5
5	2	8	9	3	7	1	4	6
1	3	6	5	4	2	9	7	8
6	7	2	3	9	5	8	1	4
8	5	4	6	7	1	2	3	9
3	1	9	8	2	4	6	5	7

201

1	7	6	8	3	4	5	9	2
8	9	2	7	1	5	6	4	3
4	5	3	6	2	9	8	1	7
9	4	1	2	5	7	3	6	8
7	3	5	1	8	6	9	2	4
2	6	8	9	4	3	7	5	1
6	8	7	4	9	2	1	3	5
5	1	4	3	6	8	2	7	9
3	2	9	5	7	1	4	8	6

202

6	1	4	2	3	8	7	9	5
7	2	5	4	6	9	3	8	1
8	3	9	7	1	5	6	2	4
9	4	8	1	2	3	5	6	7
2	5	7	6	8	4	1	3	9
3	6	1	5	9	7	8	4	2
5	7	3	8	4	2	9	1	6
1	9	2	3	5	6	4	7	8
4	8	6	9	7	1	2	5	3

203

2	3	7	9	6	8	4	1	5
8	6	1	7	4	5	2	9	3
5	9	4	3	1	2	8	7	6
4	1	8	2	9	6	5	3	7
6	2	3	1	5	7	9	8	4
7	5	9	4	8	3	6	2	1
3	7	6	8	2	4	1	5	9
9	8	5	6	3	1	7	4	2
1	4	2	5	7	9	3	6	8

204

2	8	6	1	9	7	5	3	4
5	4	7	8	6	3	2	1	9
9	3	1	4	2	5	8	6	7
8	5	9	2	3	1	7	4	6
1	6	2	9	7	4	3	8	5
4	7	3	6	5	8	9	2	1
6	9	5	3	1	2	4	7	8
3	1	4	7	8	9	6	5	2
7	2	8	5	4	6	1	9	3

205

2	9	8	3	7	4	6	5	1
6	4	1	8	9	5	3	7	2
5	3	7	2	1	6	4	8	9
1	2	5	4	8	3	9	6	7
7	6	3	1	2	9	8	4	5
9	8	4	5	6	7	2	1	3
4	1	6	7	3	2	5	9	8
3	7	9	6	5	8	1	2	4
8	5	2	9	4	1	7	3	6

206

8	5	4	6	7	3	1	2	9
9	6	1	4	5	2	3	8	7
3	7	2	9	1	8	4	5	6
5	4	7	3	9	1	8	6	2
2	3	6	5	8	7	9	1	4
1	9	8	2	6	4	7	3	5
7	2	3	1	4	6	5	9	8
6	8	9	7	3	5	2	4	1
4	1	5	8	2	9	6	7	3

207

5	6	4	3	1	9	7	2	8
3	8	1	5	7	2	6	9	4
7	2	9	6	8	4	3	1	5
1	7	6	8	5	3	9	4	2
2	4	3	7	9	1	8	5	6
8	9	5	4	2	6	1	3	7
9	5	8	1	4	7	2	6	3
4	3	2	9	6	8	5	7	1
6	1	7	2	3	5	4	8	9

208

8	9	7	1	5	3	6	4	2
2	1	6	9	7	4	3	8	5
3	5	4	8	6	2	1	7	9
4	8	1	3	9	6	2	5	7
9	6	5	7	2	1	8	3	4
7	2	3	5	4	8	9	1	6
1	7	2	4	3	9	5	6	8
6	4	8	2	1	5	7	9	3
5	3	9	6	8	7	4	2	1

209

7	5	3	2	4	1	8	9	6
6	4	2	8	9	3	5	7	1
8	1	9	5	6	7	3	4	2
1	6	5	4	8	9	2	3	7
4	3	7	1	5	2	6	8	9
9	2	8	3	7	6	1	5	4
2	8	4	9	1	5	7	6	3
3	9	6	7	2	8	4	1	5
5	7	1	6	3	4	9	2	8

210

2	4	1	8	9	5	6	3	7
8	9	3	2	6	7	5	1	4
7	5	6	3	4	1	2	8	9
9	7	8	6	5	4	3	2	1
6	3	4	9	1	2	8	7	5
5	1	2	7	3	8	9	4	6
4	8	5	1	2	6	7	9	3
1	2	9	5	7	3	4	6	8
3	6	7	4	8	9	1	5	2

211

4	7	9	8	3	1	6	2	5
2	3	1	4	6	5	7	8	9
8	5	6	9	7	2	1	3	4
7	1	4	6	9	8	2	5	3
9	8	2	5	1	3	4	6	7
5	6	3	7	2	4	9	1	8
1	4	7	3	5	6	8	9	2
3	2	8	1	4	9	5	7	6
6	9	5	2	8	7	3	4	1

212

1	3	5	7	9	8	4	6	2
2	6	9	4	5	3	7	8	1
7	8	4	6	1	2	9	5	3
5	1	3	9	2	6	8	7	4
8	2	6	5	7	4	1	3	9
4	9	7	8	3	1	5	2	6
6	4	2	1	8	5	3	9	7
3	7	8	2	4	9	6	1	5
9	5	1	3	6	7	2	4	8

213

1	2	3	4	5	6	8	9	7
4	5	9	1	7	8	6	3	2
7	8	6	2	3	9	5	1	4
2	7	5	8	4	1	9	6	3
6	9	4	5	2	3	1	7	8
8	3	1	9	6	7	2	4	5
3	1	8	7	9	5	4	2	6
9	6	2	3	8	4	7	5	1
5	4	7	6	1	2	3	8	9

214

2	4	6	8	5	7	9	3	1
3	5	8	9	1	4	2	6	7
7	1	9	2	3	6	4	8	5
5	2	4	7	6	1	8	9	3
9	3	7	5	4	8	1	2	6
6	8	1	3	9	2	7	5	4
4	6	3	1	2	9	5	7	8
1	7	2	6	8	5	3	4	9
8	9	5	4	7	3	6	1	2

215

2	3	9	6	8	4	5	1	7
4	5	7	3	9	1	8	2	6
6	8	1	7	2	5	4	9	3
1	4	2	5	6	8	7	3	9
5	9	8	2	7	3	6	4	1
3	7	6	1	4	9	2	5	8
7	2	3	9	5	6	1	8	4
9	6	4	8	1	2	3	7	5
8	1	5	4	3	7	9	6	2

216

1	7	9	6	8	2	3	4	5
4	6	5	3	7	1	2	9	8
2	3	8	9	4	5	6	1	7
5	4	2	8	6	9	1	7	3
7	8	1	2	3	4	5	6	9
3	9	6	5	1	7	8	2	4
6	5	7	1	9	3	4	8	2
9	1	3	4	2	8	7	5	6
8	2	4	7	5	6	9	3	1

217

6	4	5	9	2	3	1	7	8
1	3	7	6	8	5	2	4	9
2	8	9	4	7	1	6	5	3
8	9	6	7	5	4	3	1	2
3	1	4	2	6	9	5	8	7
5	7	2	1	3	8	4	9	6
9	6	3	5	4	7	8	2	1
7	5	8	3	1	2	9	6	4
4	2	1	8	9	6	7	3	5

218

4	7	5	2	9	6	8	3	1
3	1	9	7	5	8	4	2	6
2	6	8	1	4	3	5	9	7
5	2	1	8	3	9	7	6	4
7	3	4	6	2	1	9	8	5
8	9	6	5	7	4	2	1	3
1	5	2	3	8	7	6	4	9
6	4	7	9	1	2	3	5	8
9	8	3	4	6	5	1	7	2

219

4	6	9	7	1	8	5	3	2
8	1	3	5	9	2	6	7	4
5	7	2	3	4	6	8	9	1
6	8	5	2	7	9	4	1	3
7	9	4	1	8	3	2	6	5
3	2	1	6	5	4	9	8	7
1	4	8	9	2	7	3	5	6
2	5	6	8	3	1	7	4	9
9	3	7	4	6	5	1	2	8

220

3	1	5	4	7	6	8	9	2
6	8	2	3	9	1	5	7	4
7	4	9	8	2	5	3	1	6
2	5	7	9	6	8	1	4	3
4	9	1	5	3	2	7	6	8
8	3	6	1	4	7	2	5	9
1	2	3	6	5	4	9	8	7
9	6	8	7	1	3	4	2	5
5	7	4	2	8	9	6	3	1

221

6	7	9	2	4	5	8	3	1
8	4	2	7	3	1	5	6	9
5	1	3	9	6	8	2	4	7
9	6	7	3	8	2	1	5	4
1	8	5	4	9	6	3	7	2
2	3	4	5	1	7	9	8	6
7	5	6	8	2	9	4	1	3
3	2	1	6	5	4	7	9	8
4	9	8	1	7	3	6	2	5

222

9	8	5	2	4	1	7	3	6
4	6	1	5	7	3	9	2	8
7	2	3	6	8	9	4	1	5
1	3	7	9	6	5	8	4	2
8	9	6	1	2	4	3	5	7
2	5	4	8	3	7	1	6	9
6	1	2	4	9	8	5	7	3
5	7	8	3	1	2	6	9	4
3	4	9	7	5	6	2	8	1

223

5	3	1	7	8	9	4	6	2
9	8	7	6	4	2	3	1	5
6	4	2	5	1	3	7	8	9
2	6	9	8	7	4	1	5	3
8	7	3	1	2	5	9	4	6
4	1	5	3	9	6	8	2	7
1	5	8	2	3	7	6	9	4
7	9	6	4	5	8	2	3	1
3	2	4	9	6	1	5	7	8

224

6	2	4	9	8	7	3	1	5
5	1	3	4	2	6	9	7	8
7	8	9	3	5	1	6	2	4
2	4	1	8	9	5	7	6	3
8	3	7	6	4	2	5	9	1
9	6	5	1	7	3	4	8	2
3	7	6	5	1	8	2	4	9
1	9	2	7	3	4	8	5	6
4	5	8	2	6	9	1	3	7

225

2	1	8	4	3	6	9	5	7
6	3	9	5	7	2	8	4	1
4	5	7	8	1	9	2	6	3
9	2	5	7	6	4	1	3	8
7	6	3	1	5	8	4	9	2
8	4	1	2	9	3	5	7	6
1	9	4	3	2	7	6	8	5
5	7	6	9	8	1	3	2	4
3	8	2	6	4	5	7	1	9

226

9	5	7	8	4	6	1	2	3
8	3	2	9	7	1	4	5	6
6	1	4	2	5	3	7	8	9
3	7	5	1	6	8	2	9	4
1	9	6	3	2	4	8	7	5
2	4	8	5	9	7	3	6	1
4	6	3	7	8	9	5	1	2
5	8	9	4	1	2	6	3	7
7	2	1	6	3	5	9	4	8

227

6	1	7	2	3	8	9	5	4
8	2	5	6	4	9	3	1	7
4	9	3	5	1	7	2	8	6
3	7	6	8	2	1	4	9	5
9	8	1	3	5	4	6	7	2
5	4	2	9	7	6	8	3	1
1	3	8	4	6	5	7	2	9
2	5	4	7	9	3	1	6	8
7	6	9	1	8	2	5	4	3

228

9	3	5	6	4	1	7	2	8
2	7	6	5	9	8	3	4	1
8	4	1	2	7	3	9	5	6
7	1	9	4	5	6	8	3	2
6	5	3	9	8	2	1	7	4
4	8	2	1	3	7	6	9	5
1	6	7	3	2	5	4	8	9
3	2	4	8	1	9	5	6	7
5	9	8	7	6	4	2	1	3

229

3	1	6	5	9	4	7	2	8
7	5	4	8	3	2	9	1	6
8	2	9	7	6	1	5	3	4
6	7	2	3	8	5	4	9	1
1	3	5	9	4	6	8	7	2
4	9	8	1	2	7	3	6	5
9	6	3	4	1	8	2	5	7
5	4	1	2	7	9	6	8	3
2	8	7	6	5	3	1	4	9

230

2	5	1	8	6	4	9	7	3
4	8	3	1	7	9	6	5	2
9	7	6	3	2	5	4	1	8
7	4	9	5	8	1	3	2	6
1	2	5	6	4	3	8	9	7
3	6	8	7	9	2	1	4	5
6	9	2	4	5	8	7	3	1
8	1	4	2	3	7	5	6	9
5	3	7	9	1	6	2	8	4

231

5	3	1	8	2	9	6	4	7
4	9	7	6	3	5	8	1	2
8	6	2	4	1	7	3	5	9
7	5	3	9	4	1	2	6	8
1	8	6	2	5	3	9	7	4
2	4	9	7	8	6	1	3	5
3	1	8	5	9	4	7	2	6
9	7	5	3	6	2	4	8	1
6	2	4	1	7	8	5	9	3

232

9	6	8	5	2	4	7	3	1
4	1	2	7	6	3	5	9	8
3	5	7	1	9	8	4	2	6
8	2	6	3	7	1	9	4	5
5	4	3	6	8	9	2	1	7
7	9	1	4	5	2	6	8	3
2	3	5	8	4	7	1	6	9
1	7	9	2	3	6	8	5	4
6	8	4	9	1	5	3	7	2

Puzzle 233

5	4	2	6	9	7	1	3	8
6	3	8	2	1	4	5	9	7
9	1	7	5	3	8	4	6	2
3	5	6	1	7	2	8	4	9
8	7	1	9	4	5	3	2	6
2	9	4	8	6	3	7	5	1
4	8	9	7	5	6	2	1	3
7	6	5	3	2	1	9	8	4
1	2	3	4	8	9	6	7	5

Puzzle 234

6	2	5	3	4	8	7	9	1
1	4	3	9	7	6	8	5	2
7	8	9	5	1	2	6	4	3
9	1	4	8	2	7	5	3	6
5	6	8	1	9	3	4	2	7
3	7	2	4	6	5	9	1	8
8	3	1	7	5	9	2	6	4
2	9	7	6	3	4	1	8	5
4	5	6	2	8	1	3	7	9

Puzzle 235

9	8	2	1	6	5	4	7	3
7	4	1	9	2	3	8	6	5
5	6	3	7	4	8	1	2	9
8	9	6	5	7	1	3	4	2
3	2	5	4	8	6	9	1	7
4	1	7	3	9	2	6	5	8
6	5	9	8	1	7	2	3	4
1	7	8	2	3	4	5	9	6
2	3	4	6	5	9	7	8	1

Puzzle 236

9	7	4	3	5	8	1	6	2
2	6	8	9	4	1	7	5	3
1	3	5	7	6	2	8	9	4
8	4	6	5	1	3	9	2	7
5	1	9	2	7	4	6	3	8
3	2	7	8	9	6	5	4	1
4	8	1	6	3	5	2	7	9
7	5	2	4	8	9	3	1	6
6	9	3	1	2	7	4	8	5

Puzzle 237

6	7	2	4	1	8	5	3	9
4	9	1	2	5	3	6	8	7
8	5	3	9	7	6	1	2	4
2	3	6	7	8	9	4	5	1
7	8	4	5	2	1	9	6	3
5	1	9	6	3	4	8	7	2
3	4	5	1	6	7	2	9	8
9	2	8	3	4	5	7	1	6
1	6	7	8	9	2	3	4	5

Puzzle 238

6	8	4	3	7	1	5	2	9
1	2	3	6	9	5	4	7	8
7	9	5	2	8	4	3	1	6
4	1	7	9	6	3	8	5	2
8	3	9	7	5	2	6	4	1
2	5	6	1	4	8	9	3	7
9	6	2	4	3	7	1	8	5
3	7	8	5	1	9	2	6	4
5	4	1	8	2	6	7	9	3

Puzzle 239

6	8	4	2	5	7	1	3	9
2	9	7	1	6	3	8	4	5
3	5	1	8	9	4	6	2	7
1	2	9	3	4	5	7	6	8
4	7	3	6	1	8	9	5	2
8	6	5	7	2	9	4	1	3
7	3	2	4	8	6	5	9	1
9	1	6	5	7	2	3	8	4
5	4	8	9	3	1	2	7	6

Puzzle 240

1	6	8	2	9	5	3	7	4
4	2	7	6	1	3	8	9	5
5	9	3	8	4	7	2	6	1
2	8	1	4	7	9	5	3	6
3	7	6	1	5	2	9	4	8
9	4	5	3	8	6	1	2	7
8	1	2	9	6	4	7	5	3
6	5	9	7	3	1	4	8	2
7	3	4	5	2	8	6	1	9

Puzzle 241

9	3	4	8	7	2	1	6	5
5	8	1	3	6	9	4	7	2
6	2	7	5	4	1	9	8	3
7	5	9	6	1	8	2	3	4
2	4	3	9	5	7	6	1	8
1	6	8	2	3	4	5	9	7
8	7	2	1	9	5	3	4	6
3	1	5	4	8	6	7	2	9
4	9	6	7	2	3	8	5	1

Puzzle 242

4	2	3	8	7	9	6	5	1
8	1	9	3	6	5	2	4	7
7	6	5	4	1	2	3	9	8
3	4	8	6	5	7	9	1	2
2	5	6	9	4	1	8	7	3
1	9	7	2	3	8	4	6	5
9	8	1	7	2	6	5	3	4
5	3	2	1	9	4	7	8	6
6	7	4	5	8	3	1	2	9

Puzzle 243

4	5	8	1	9	6	7	2	3
6	7	1	4	2	3	5	8	9
2	9	3	5	8	7	4	1	6
9	1	7	6	4	2	3	5	8
3	2	5	8	1	9	6	4	7
8	6	4	7	3	5	2	9	1
1	4	6	2	7	8	9	3	5
7	3	2	9	5	1	8	6	4
5	8	9	3	6	4	1	7	2

Puzzle 244

7	9	5	1	8	4	2	3	6
6	1	8	3	2	9	5	7	4
3	4	2	5	7	6	9	1	8
9	6	4	2	5	3	7	8	1
2	5	7	6	1	8	4	9	3
1	8	3	4	9	7	6	2	5
4	2	6	7	3	1	8	5	9
8	7	1	9	6	5	3	4	2
5	3	9	8	4	2	1	6	7

Puzzle 245

4	2	9	6	5	3	8	1	7
1	6	8	2	7	9	3	5	4
3	5	7	1	4	8	6	9	2
7	9	4	3	1	6	5	2	8
5	3	2	8	9	7	4	6	1
8	1	6	4	2	5	7	3	9
6	4	3	9	8	1	2	7	5
2	7	1	5	6	4	9	8	3
9	8	5	7	3	2	1	4	6

Puzzle 246

4	1	7	5	6	8	3	2	9
5	6	8	3	9	2	7	1	4
9	2	3	4	7	1	8	6	5
6	8	2	7	1	5	4	9	3
3	7	5	9	2	4	6	8	1
1	9	4	6	8	3	2	5	7
8	4	9	2	5	7	1	3	6
2	3	6	1	4	9	5	7	8
7	5	1	8	3	6	9	4	2

Puzzle 247

9	3	8	6	1	7	2	4	5
2	5	4	3	8	9	6	7	1
7	1	6	2	5	4	3	8	9
1	2	9	5	6	8	7	3	4
5	8	3	4	7	2	9	1	6
6	4	7	9	3	1	8	5	2
3	7	5	1	2	6	4	9	8
4	6	1	8	9	3	5	2	7
8	9	2	7	4	5	1	6	3

Puzzle 248

7	8	4	2	1	3	6	9	5
3	9	6	5	4	7	8	2	1
2	5	1	6	8	9	7	3	4
9	1	5	7	6	2	4	8	3
4	6	3	8	5	1	2	7	9
8	7	2	9	3	4	5	1	6
1	3	8	4	2	5	9	6	7
5	2	7	1	9	6	3	4	8
6	4	9	3	7	8	1	5	2

249

7	3	5	2	6	9	8	4	1
9	1	6	7	4	8	3	5	2
4	8	2	5	1	3	9	7	6
6	9	7	8	2	4	5	1	3
8	4	1	9	3	5	6	2	7
2	5	3	6	7	1	4	9	8
5	2	8	3	9	7	1	6	4
1	6	9	4	8	2	7	3	5
3	7	4	1	5	6	2	8	9

250

2	4	5	7	6	8	1	3	9
3	1	6	9	2	4	8	5	7
9	8	7	1	5	3	6	2	4
7	5	1	3	4	9	2	8	6
4	2	9	5	8	6	7	1	3
6	3	8	2	1	7	4	9	5
1	7	4	8	3	5	9	6	2
5	9	2	6	7	1	3	4	8
8	6	3	4	9	2	5	7	1

251

6	2	7	4	3	1	8	5	9
3	1	5	8	9	6	7	2	4
8	4	9	5	7	2	6	1	3
1	8	3	6	4	9	5	7	2
7	5	6	2	8	3	9	4	1
2	9	4	7	1	5	3	8	6
5	7	1	9	6	4	2	3	8
4	6	8	3	2	7	1	9	5
9	3	2	1	5	8	4	6	7

252

8	5	4	6	1	7	2	3	9
9	6	7	5	2	3	1	4	8
3	1	2	9	8	4	5	6	7
5	9	6	4	3	8	7	1	2
7	3	8	1	9	2	6	5	4
2	4	1	7	5	6	9	8	3
4	8	9	2	6	1	3	7	5
6	7	5	3	4	9	8	2	1
1	2	3	8	7	5	4	9	6

253

8	2	1	6	9	5	3	4	7
4	9	6	8	3	7	2	1	5
3	5	7	4	1	2	9	6	8
1	4	2	3	7	8	5	9	6
7	3	8	9	5	6	1	2	4
9	6	5	1	2	4	7	8	3
5	7	4	2	8	9	6	3	1
6	1	9	5	4	3	8	7	2
2	8	3	7	6	1	4	5	9

254

4	7	3	1	6	8	2	5	9
8	9	2	4	7	5	1	3	6
1	5	6	9	2	3	4	7	8
5	1	9	6	4	2	3	8	7
3	8	4	7	5	1	9	6	2
6	2	7	8	3	9	5	4	1
9	4	8	5	1	6	7	2	3
7	3	1	2	8	4	6	9	5
2	6	5	3	9	7	8	1	4

255

6	2	1	8	3	4	9	5	7
4	3	7	5	1	9	6	2	8
8	5	9	7	2	6	4	3	1
1	9	3	2	5	8	7	6	4
7	8	4	1	6	3	5	9	2
2	6	5	9	4	7	1	8	3
9	1	8	3	7	5	2	4	6
5	7	6	4	8	2	3	1	9
3	4	2	6	9	1	8	7	5

256

1	8	4	3	2	6	9	5	7
2	6	5	4	7	9	3	1	8
3	9	7	8	5	1	6	4	2
4	7	6	1	3	2	8	9	5
5	1	3	6	9	8	2	7	4
8	2	9	5	4	7	1	6	3
9	3	8	7	1	4	5	2	6
6	4	1	2	8	5	7	3	9
7	5	2	9	6	3	4	8	1

257

9	7	3	4	2	1	8	5	6
8	2	1	3	5	6	4	9	7
4	5	6	7	9	8	2	3	1
2	8	9	1	4	5	6	7	3
7	1	5	8	6	3	9	4	2
6	3	4	2	7	9	1	8	5
3	9	8	5	1	2	7	6	4
1	6	7	9	3	4	5	2	8
5	4	2	6	8	7	3	1	9

258

1	7	2	8	3	6	4	9	5
8	4	9	7	5	2	3	6	1
5	3	6	4	1	9	8	2	7
4	2	3	6	9	7	1	5	8
7	5	1	3	2	8	9	4	6
9	6	8	1	4	5	2	7	3
6	9	5	2	8	1	7	3	4
2	8	4	5	7	3	6	1	9
3	1	7	9	6	4	5	8	2

259

1	5	3	2	4	7	6	9	8
6	8	9	3	5	1	7	2	4
2	7	4	8	6	9	3	1	5
8	9	5	1	2	6	4	3	7
3	6	2	5	7	4	9	8	1
7	4	1	9	3	8	2	5	6
4	3	8	6	1	2	5	7	9
9	2	7	4	8	5	1	6	3
5	1	6	7	9	3	8	4	2

260

5	7	4	6	3	8	2	9	1
1	3	2	7	9	5	4	6	8
6	9	8	4	1	2	7	5	3
3	4	6	1	8	7	5	2	9
2	8	1	9	5	4	3	7	6
9	5	7	2	6	3	8	1	4
8	1	5	3	2	6	9	4	7
4	2	9	8	7	1	6	3	5
7	6	3	5	4	9	1	8	2

261

5	3	9	1	7	4	8	6	2
8	6	7	5	3	2	4	9	1
4	1	2	9	8	6	3	5	7
6	5	8	7	4	9	1	2	3
3	7	4	2	6	1	9	8	5
9	2	1	3	5	8	6	7	4
2	8	5	4	9	3	7	1	6
7	9	3	6	1	5	2	4	8
1	4	6	8	2	7	5	3	9

262

3	9	5	6	8	4	1	2	7
1	6	2	7	3	9	4	8	5
8	4	7	5	1	2	9	6	3
4	2	9	8	6	7	3	5	1
6	1	8	4	5	3	2	7	9
7	5	3	2	9	1	8	4	6
5	7	1	3	2	8	6	9	4
2	3	6	9	4	5	7	1	8
9	8	4	1	7	6	5	3	2

263

6	3	1	8	4	2	5	7	9
5	8	4	7	3	9	2	6	1
7	9	2	1	5	6	4	3	8
4	1	9	3	6	7	8	2	5
3	6	8	4	2	5	9	1	7
2	5	7	9	8	1	3	4	6
9	2	5	6	1	4	7	8	3
1	4	3	5	7	8	6	9	2
8	7	6	2	9	3	1	5	4

264

3	5	2	6	8	7	9	4	1
8	7	9	1	2	4	3	5	6
6	4	1	5	9	3	2	7	8
7	8	4	9	6	5	1	2	3
2	3	6	8	4	1	5	9	7
1	9	5	7	3	2	6	8	4
5	2	7	4	1	6	8	3	9
9	6	3	2	7	8	4	1	5
4	1	8	3	5	9	7	6	2

265

5	7	8	1	2	4	6	3	9
4	9	3	7	5	6	1	2	8
1	6	2	9	3	8	4	7	5
8	3	5	2	7	1	9	4	6
7	4	1	3	6	9	5	8	2
9	2	6	8	4	5	7	1	3
2	5	7	4	9	3	8	6	1
3	8	9	6	1	7	2	5	4
6	1	4	5	8	2	3	9	7

266

4	9	1	3	2	6	7	8	5
8	5	7	4	1	9	2	3	6
6	3	2	8	5	7	1	4	9
7	4	6	2	3	5	9	1	8
9	2	3	7	8	1	6	5	4
5	1	8	9	6	4	3	2	7
1	8	4	6	7	3	5	9	2
3	6	9	5	4	2	8	7	1
2	7	5	1	9	8	4	6	3

267

3	9	2	5	8	1	4	7	6
7	6	1	2	9	4	8	5	3
5	8	4	7	3	6	2	9	1
9	7	5	3	6	8	1	2	4
1	2	8	9	4	5	6	3	7
6	4	3	1	7	2	5	8	9
8	3	6	4	2	7	9	1	5
4	5	9	8	1	3	7	6	2
2	1	7	6	5	9	3	4	8

268

9	7	5	2	8	4	1	6	3
8	1	6	9	7	3	4	5	2
2	3	4	1	6	5	8	9	7
6	5	9	3	4	7	2	8	1
4	8	3	6	2	1	5	7	9
1	2	7	5	9	8	3	4	6
5	6	2	8	3	9	7	1	4
7	9	8	4	1	2	6	3	5
3	4	1	7	5	6	9	2	8

269

7	5	9	2	6	4	1	8	3
6	3	4	5	8	1	7	9	2
8	2	1	7	9	3	6	5	4
1	7	2	9	3	8	4	6	5
4	8	5	1	2	6	9	3	7
9	6	3	4	5	7	2	1	8
5	1	7	8	4	9	3	2	6
2	4	6	3	1	5	8	7	9
3	9	8	6	7	2	5	4	1

270

9	4	1	2	6	8	5	7	3
3	8	5	7	9	4	1	6	2
6	2	7	3	1	5	9	8	4
7	5	3	4	2	9	8	1	6
1	6	2	8	3	7	4	9	5
8	9	4	1	5	6	3	2	7
5	7	6	9	4	1	2	3	8
2	1	8	5	7	3	6	4	9
4	3	9	6	8	2	7	5	1

271

7	4	2	3	1	9	5	8	6
9	6	1	7	8	5	3	2	4
3	8	5	4	2	6	7	9	1
1	3	6	9	7	8	2	4	5
5	7	8	2	3	4	1	6	9
2	9	4	5	6	1	8	7	3
6	2	7	1	4	3	9	5	8
8	5	3	6	9	2	4	1	7
4	1	9	8	5	7	6	3	2

272

3	1	2	9	7	6	5	4	8
4	9	8	3	2	5	7	1	6
6	7	5	4	1	8	2	3	9
5	4	7	8	6	1	9	2	3
1	6	9	5	3	2	4	8	7
2	8	3	7	4	9	1	6	5
9	2	4	6	5	3	8	7	1
8	3	1	2	9	7	6	5	4
7	5	6	1	8	4	3	9	2